GODS, GIANTS & the GEOGRAPHY of INDIA

Nalini Ramachandran is always looking for interesting stories to tell – of glorious goddesses, daunting demons, stealthy shape-shifters, gorgeous geographies, wondrous wildlife, inspirational innovators and ordinary objects. Her works, both fiction and non-fiction, have appeared in a range of formats: comics and graphic novels, newspaper articles and magazine features, short stories and school textbooks, children's books and coffee-table books, animation scripts and screenplays. She also conducts workshops on creative writing and storytelling. To know more about her, visit www.authornalini.com.

NALINI RAMACHANDRAN

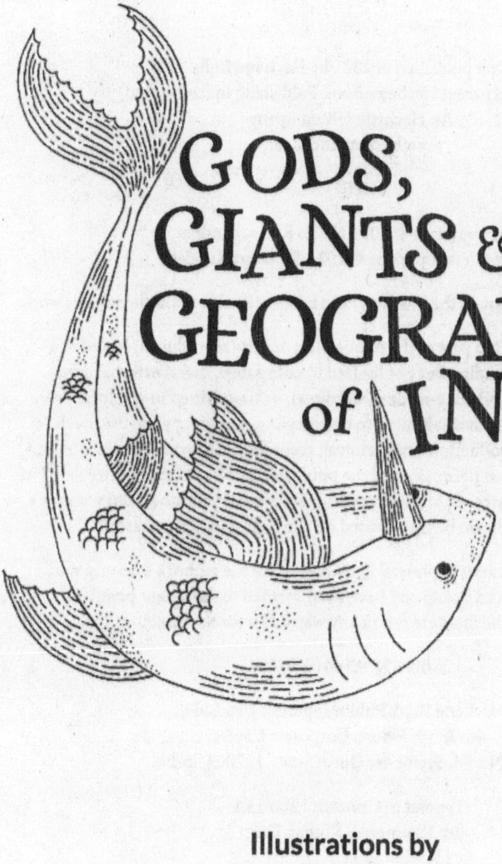

GODS, GIANTS & the GEOGRAPHY of INDIA

Illustrations by
Sharanya Kunnath

First published in 2021 by Hachette India
(Registered name: Hachette Book Publishing India Pvt. Ltd)
An Hachette UK company
www.hachetteindia.com

SRD

ISBN 978-93-91028-22-0

Hachette Book Publishing India Pvt. Ltd
4th & 5th Floors, Corporate Centre
Plot No. 94, Sector 44, Gurugram – 122003, India

Typeset in Crimson 12.5/15.8
by Manmohan Kumar, Delhi

Printed and bound in India
by Manipal Technologies Limited

Contents

Author's Note

The Intriguing World of Geography

Deep below the outermost layer of the earth, unseen by all of us, lives a mysterious race of human beings. Every once in a while, just to check if the humans inhabiting the earth's crust are still around, they pound at the earth's insides with great force. The ground groans loudly and shakes dangerously. At such a time, if the ones residing on the surface of the earth scream, 'We're alive! We're alive!' the hidden humans stop their thumping. Just one shout is enough to let them know that we are still living on the other side.

This is not a story I just made up. It's a folktale from Assam about how earthquakes are caused and why sometimes the tremors stop soon after. Generations of different communities have passed on several such stories orally to their children and grandchildren. It is through this enchanting realm of folklore that early humans tried to make sense of mysterious geographical events like earthquakes, volcanoes, avalanches and floods, and geological formations like mountains, valleys, glaciers and caves. Over time, even though these beliefs have made way for scientific knowledge, folktales continue to be told.

If you travel to a hilly region today, the first thing you'd get to know about the place is not the type of rocks found there or the scientific process that causes a peak's volcanic activity. Instead, you are more likely to come across the story of how a balancing rock, placed there by a divine being, still stands steady at a particular angle, or how a giant who lives inside the mountain spews fire through its peak when he is angry.

Not all stories are mere figments of people's imagination. Some mythologists say that there is a fair amount of scientific truth hidden in many of these tales, because they do describe how certain geographical events occurred years ago or how specific places came to exist.

For example, an important episode in the Ramayana narrates how the mighty Hanuman found a life-giving herb in a mountainous region, which saved the life of Prince Lakshmana. Happy with Hanuman's deed, the gods showered him with hundreds of different kinds of flowers, in gorgeous hues and with soothing fragrances, from the heavens. These fallen flowers turned that mountainous area into one of the most exquisite gardens in the world. The Valley of Flowers in Uttarakhand is believed to be the very place where this scene took place. Today, botanists have found that the region is home to around 500 different types of flowering plants and more than 100 types of medicinal plants. A rare natural wonder, the valley has now earned the UNESCO World Heritage Site tag!

These tales remind me of how different geography was in school. At that time, making and marking maps was the only thing I enjoyed in class – maybe because I loved drawing. I would obsess over getting the minute details in the outlines of the Indian states and union territories right – they had to look like a well-joined jigsaw puzzle, after all. Using different symbols and coloured pencils to plot rivers, mountains, forests and deserts on those maps was also a lot of fun. Once I even created an agricultural map of India for a class project by sticking actual grains and pulses, swabs of cotton and bits of jute on it to indicate where these crops grew. But the fascinating connections between myths and real places and processes made me realize that there was much more to geography than just maps.

So, I dug around for more and more stories and discovered that the myths and legends which tell us about the geography of a place through characters such as gods and giants make up the sphere of what is called 'geomythology'. A combination of the words 'geography' or 'geology' and 'mythology', this term was coined by the geologist Dorothy B. Vitaliano in 1968. However, some of the most referred dictionaries are yet to include geomythology as a valid English word.

The more research I did, the more determined I was to present India's geography in a new avatar – in the form of stories! And that is why I decided to write this book and introduce the intriguing world of Indian geomythology to you lovely readers. The book is much more than a random collection of geomyths. I have picked tales that have interesting characters and lots of action, and which also present the diverse landscape of the country. These stories are a unique record of human evolution and cultural beliefs. Most importantly, they call attention to climate change and how the world is slowly disintegrating. In essence, they are rooted in creation, preservation and destruction – the very themes that bind mythology and geography.

Not all Indian geomyths are a part of this book – there are way too many, and each myth has multiple versions. Once you finish reading, maybe you could go myth-hunting too and share what you find with me. If you love maps as much as I do, you could even create your own geomythological map of India.

Until then, sit back and enjoy these splendid stories about India and the earth that is our home. And oh, the next time you feel the ground shaking suddenly, you know what's going on!

Where the Gods Live

Where do the gods live? All the stories tell us that it's either in the sky or some version of heaven. But often, these divine beings have been known to travel through and even live on earth for a while (or eternity, in some cases), either because they want a change of scene, or to vanquish a havoc-wreaking villain, or to simply find a quiet place to meditate in.

The holy trinity from Hindu mythology – Brahma (the creator of the universe), Vishnu (the preserver) and Shiva (the destroyer) – too have second homes on Prithvi Lok (the world of humans). Turns out, even the most powerful gods in the universe can't resist the call of the mountains...

1

Under the Giant Jambu Tree

Jambudvipa

'Whoa!' Batara Guru sat up and looked around. Something had violently shaken him awake. 'Great. The ground's moving and tilting *again*,' he sighed.

Batara Guru was the chief god of a floating island called Javadvipa. Not too long ago, he had made a request to his friends Brahma and Vishnu, who were the chief gods of the neighbouring island of Jambudvipa. 'Send some humans over to reside on Javadvipa too, please!' he had told them.

Brahma and Vishnu agreed, and settled a large group of people on Javadvipa. Batara Guru was happy.

But soon, Javadvipa began facing a peculiar problem. Since it was a floating island, its surface was very wobbly – it moved about all the time. Now that the island's inhabitants had grown in number, Batara Guru found it difficult to keep Javadvipa steady. Sometimes, the island tilted this way; sometimes, it sloped that way. And with it, all its inhabitants went sliding down too, until Batara

Guru saved them from falling into the ocean below. It was complete chaos!

'Whoa, whoa, whoa!' shouted Batara Guru, when he felt the ground move yet again.

'There's only one solution now,' he muttered to himself, trying to keep his balance. '*Vishnuuuuu*! *Brahmaaaaa*!' he called out.

Brahma, the creator of the Brahmanda, or the cosmos, was busy sipping his favourite juice. 'Umm…delicious as always!' he said. This dark purple juice came directly from the Jambunadi, a river that flowed through the island of Jambudvipa.

The waters of the Jambunadi, in turn, came from the fruits of the gigantic *jambu* tree. So huge was this tree that each berry on it was as big as a full-grown elephant! When these ripe fruits fell on the hard ground with a resounding *splosh*, gallons and gallons of juice flowed out in the form of Jambunadi. Everyone who lived around it, including Brahma, merrily drank from it. It is not surprising then that Jambudvipa was named after *jambu* – the most loved fruit on the island.

At the centre of Jambudvipa stood Meru, an upside-down golden mountain. Floating above Mount Meru was Brahmapuri, the glistening city of Brahma. Hovering way above it was Satya Lok, the god's other divine realm. But he much preferred the view of the island from his seat atop Meru. And that's where he sat now, surveying every corner of Jambudvipa (he had four heads, so that was easy!).

'So beautiful my Bhu Mandala looks!' Brahma said.

A part of the Brahmanda, Bhu Mandala (also called Prithvi Lok) was made up of seven oceans and seven *dvipa,* meaning 'islands' or 'continents'. These formed alternating concentric circles – one ring of ocean, followed by a ring of land, and so on. But there was a time when Bhu Mandala was a single, large landmass, and not a group of separate islands.

Once, Brahma's grandson, Priyavrata, rode his chariot over this land as he followed the sun. He was circumambulating (or circling around) Mount Meru, which stood at the centre of this mass. The wheels of his chariot created seven deep, circular ditches, which later became the seven oceans. The lands between them became the seven *dvipa*.

Six of these islands were shaped like rings, but Jambudvipa alone resembled a disc, because it was the innermost island. Mountain ranges further separated Jambudvipa into nine regions. The southernmost of these regions, which was bordered by the Himavan Mountains, was called Bharat.

Brahma was still smiling to himself, as he sipped his *jambu* juice, when he saw Vishnu rushing towards him. 'What a pleasant surprise!' he remarked.

'Looks like you've been lost in your own world again,' Vishnu said. 'Batara Guru has been calling us.'

'Oh! Has he?' Brahma asked, clearly clueless. 'What happened?'

Vishnu shrugged as the two of them immediately made their way to the neighbouring island of Javadvipa.

An anxious Batara Guru welcomed his friends. 'What took you both so long?' he asked.

Vishnu glanced sideways at Brahma. Not waiting for a response, Batara Guru continued, 'Javadvipa moves and shakes all the time. With all the movement of the humans living on it as well now, it's just getting worse. I want you to help me fix the island in one place.'

Vishnu thought aloud, 'That makes sense. But how do we do this?'

'Use Mount Meru!' Batara Guru replied.

Vishnu went quiet, for he knew how much Brahma loved the golden mountain. But to his surprise, the god of creation readily agreed.

And so, back in Jambudvipa, the two gods broke a large chunk off the lofty Meru. Vishnu transformed himself into a giant turtle, and Brahma placed the mountain block on his shell.

'It's better to fasten the rock, or else it might slide off your smooth back,' Brahma said. Taking the form of a giant snake, he wound himself tightly around the rock and the turtle so that they wouldn't move. 'We're ready to go, Vishnu!' he said.

Soon, the two gods arrived at Javadvipa with the huge wedge of Mount Meru. 'Wait, where do we fix this?' Brahma asked.

'Let's put it down here,' Vishnu said. But Brahma insisted on dragging it in another direction.

'Oh, just place it somewhere...anywhere!' an exasperated Batara Guru said, throwing his hands up in the air.

By the time the gods could agree on a spot, bits and pieces from the large chunk of Meru crumbled and fell across the surface of Javadvipa. These became smaller mountains in themselves.

'Ah, there!' Brahma and Vishnu announced in unison as they finally agreed on a good spot. Under the weight of the newly placed rocky mass, the land sat unmoving and steady at last.

'Perfect!' said Batara Guru, and thanked Brahma and Vishnu.

'This mountain will be my new home,' he added.

Happy that they had been able to help their neighbour, the pair then headed back to their island.

'*Oww*! My back is aching!' said Vishnu, groaning as he stretched. 'Brahma, I think I need some refreshing *jambu* juice too.'

Brahma laughed heartily. That was exactly what he had in mind!

Connecting the Dots...

Jambudvipa is believed to be the ancient name for the Indian subcontinent, while the six other dvipa *are the other continents that make up the world today. The Himavan Mountains stand for the Himalayas. Apart from Hindu mythology, Buddhist and Jain creation stories also point to the existence of Jambudvipa and Mount Meru. Theories like these fall under the realm of mythological cosmology.*

Javadvipa, now known as Java Island, is a part of present-day Indonesia. According to Javanese mythology, Jambudvipa and Javadvipa are neighbouring islands. Mount Semeru, a volcanic mountain that is among the highest in Java, is said to be the legendary Mount Meru that Brahma and Vishnu brought in from Jambudvipa at the behest of Batara Guru (considered to be a form of Shiva).

Jambudvipa gets its name from jambu*, the Sanskrit name for the fruit known as jamun or the Indian blackberry. Some people believe that Jambudvipa means 'Roseapple Island', as the roseapple is called* jambu *in Sanskrit as well. Interestingly,* jambu *or jamun is also known as Java plum.*

The Many Names of India

It can be slightly confusing, but some mythologists believe that Jambudvipa denotes the earth (as it is shaped like a sphere or disc), and Bharat denotes the region where modern India is located. The Indian subcontinent came to be known as Bharat during the reign of King Bharata, who conquered the entire subcontinent and ruled over the region – so it is said in the Mahabharata.

Ancient India has been known by many intriguing names in other countries and languages as well:

- Hodu in Hebrew
- Hind/Hindustan in Persian
- Indica, as used by Megasthenes, a traveller from Greece
- Tianzhu in ancient Chinese; however, Tianzhu was pronounced Tenjiku in Japan and Cheonchuk in Korea.

The subcontinent gets its present name, India, from the River Indus, a major waterbody in the country. Did you know that even though India looks pretty small on a map, it is the seventh-largest country in the world?

Geography on a Plate

Just as Brahma's Prithvi Lok didn't have the seven *dvipa* before Priyavrata's chariot wheels broke them apart, the earth didn't always have the seven continents that we know of today. Instead, there existed an enormous mass of land, a supercontinent called Pangaea, around 290 million years ago. A mash-up of the Greek words *pan*, meaning 'all', and 'Gaia' or 'earth', Pangaea stands for 'all the earth'. This means that the seven continents, which are a part of our present-day planet, belonged to this giant landmass. At that time, all the water on the earth surrounded this landmass, and did not flow through it.

In 1912, Alfred Wegener, a geophysicist (a scientist who studies the earth's physical processes and changes), discovered that this supercontinent broke off and drifted apart over millions of years, eventually becoming seven separate continents. He called his theory the 'continental drift'.

In the 1960s, some scientists came up with another theory called 'plate tectonics'. They suggested that several thick layers or plates of land make up the earth's crust (the outermost layer of the earth). Below the crust is the mantle, followed by the outer and inner cores, which are a mixture of solid and liquid layers, made up of assorted minerals and materials.

According to the tectonic theory, the plates on the earth's crust move by one or two inches every year.

A range of tectonic movements continuously shape the world's geography. For example, when two plates grind against one another, an earthquake is caused. When one plate moves below another, mountains are formed, and so on. Interestingly, the word tectonic comes from the Greek word *tekton*, which means 'builder'. The moving plates keep building an evolving world, and changing versions of the world map are a proof of this.

A Massive Jigsaw Puzzle

At first, Pangaea broke into two landmasses – Laurasia in the northern hemisphere and Gondwanaland in the southern hemisphere. The surrounding water began flowing between these two supercontinents as the Tethys Sea. As Laurasia and Gondwanaland broke further, they formed the continents that we know of today. North America and Eurasia, which consisted of Europe and Asia (except India), emerged from Laurasia. Gondwanaland fragmented into South America, Africa, Arabia, Antarctica and Australia.

India, which was a part of Africa at that time, was separated as well. An island then, the Indian subcontinent floated on and on for 50 million years, until it collided with and joined the Eurasian continent in the northern hemisphere to become a peninsula (a mass of land bound by water on three sides). The collision of the Eurasian and Indian plates gave rise to one of the world's highest mountain ranges – the Himalayas!

Land of the Forest People

Gondwanaland has an interesting connection with India. The supercontinent gets its name from Gond *van* or the 'forests of Gond'. The Gonds are one of the largest tribes in India, who now reside in its central, eastern and southern states. In the forests where the Gonds live, geologists (scientists who study the physical features of the earth) have discovered rocks dating back to the time when this region was a part of the southern supercontinent. This discovery led geologists to name the landmass Gondwanaland after the tribe and its forests.

Just as the earth's plates move ceaselessly, divine beings too have been traversing different realms in the universe that Brahma created. Apart from them, the asuras (demons who lived in Patal Lok or the underworld), as well as some sages, could wander through the worlds at will. Did you know that a powerful asura, and later a wise sage, once forced Vishnu to leave his celestial abode and live on Prithvi Lok instead?

2

An Ornamental Arch

Silathoranam

Sage Bhrigu was flabbergasted...and somewhat embarrassed. This was *not* the reaction he had expected from Vishnu. He tried to release his foot from the god's grip, but Vishnu continued to massage it with the utmost sincerity.

Lakshmi narrowed her eyes in anger. 'You know what? I'm leaving!' she announced.

'Uh-huh... When will you be back?' Vishnu asked distractedly, not taking his eyes off Bhrigu's foot.

'Never!' said the enraged goddess and stormed out.

Long, long ago, an asura named Hiranyaksha displaced Prithvi Lok from its original position in the universe, and hid it deep inside the dark Garbhodaka Ocean, way below Patal Lok. All the beings who lived on Prithvi Lok were wiped out instantly.

A furious Vishnu took the form of a gigantic wild boar called Varaha and defeated Hiranyaksha in a long battle. Varaha then dived into the Garbhodaka Ocean and lifted up the submerged Prithvi Lok. Putting it safely back in its place, Varaha asked Brahma to create a new world with living beings all over again.

'This time, I will stay on Prithvi Lok and protect it. Let me see who tries to destroy it then!' he declared, grunting angrily.

A large hill with seven peaks on Prithvi Lok became Vishnu's second home, from where he kept a watch for many, many years. But one day, the god decided to return to Vaikunth, his celestial abode.

'This is worrisome,' Brahma confided in Narada, a travelling sage and storyteller. 'I can see that a dark era is beginning, and only Vishnu can protect Prithvi Lok and its beings. Narada, do something! Make Vishnu go back to his sacred hill home.'

The wise (and sometimes mischievous) Narada, an ardent devotee of Vishnu, set off for Prithvi Lok to fulfil his task.

There, he saw Bhrigu, along with his fellow sages, conducting a special ritual for the holy trinity of Brahma, Vishnu and Shiva. A divine fruit emerged from the sacred fire at the end of the ceremony.

The puzzled sages looked at each other. 'How do we gift a single fruit to the holy trinity?' one of them asked.

'We can't cut it, obviously!'

'Then we should just give it to only one of them.'

Needless to say, a huge argument ensued.

Bhrigu silenced them with a look. *How silly is it that wise, learned people like us are wasting time arguing about such matters!* he thought.

'Do you have a better plan?' asked another sage.

Just then, Narada made an entrance. '*Narayana, Narayana...*' he chanted. 'Why not give it to the greatest god?' he suggested with a twinkle in his eye, knowing exactly how things would pan out.

'That's a good idea, Sage Narada,' one of them said. 'But how will we know who the greatest of them is?'

'Leave that to me!' Bhrigu answered. 'I will find out who among the holy trinity is the greatest god. We must give this fruit to him and him alone!'

His work done, Narada grinned and vanished.

The other sages still looked perplexed. 'Whatever you do, make sure you don't irritate the holy trinity!' they warned Bhrigu.

But Bhrigu was too lost in his own thoughts to hear them. He took the fruit and left for Satya Lok, the abode of Brahma.

When Bhrigu encountered the god, he noticed that each of Brahma's four heads was preoccupied – one was poring over the Vedas (sacred texts containing prayers, hymns and rituals). The second was busy chanting '*Om namo Narayanaya*'. The third was conjuring up new creations for Prithvi Lok, and the fourth was intently listening to his wife, Saraswati, playing the veena, her favourite musical instrument.

'Brahmadev,' Bhrigu called out respectfully. But the busy god irritably waved him away.

A miffed Bhrigu left for Mount Kailash, the abode of Shiva. As soon as the sage left, Brahma smiled – he knew exactly what Narada had set in motion.

On Mount Kailash, Bhrigu found that the god was deep in conversation with his wife.

'Mahadev,' the sage called out politely. Shiva glared at him in response. He looked like he was about to turn Bhrigu to ashes for having intruded into his personal space.

An annoyed Bhrigu then headed to Vaikunth, the abode of Vishnu.

After a long argument with the gatekeepers, who finally let him in, he came upon Vishnu resting blissfully on the coiled Sheshnag, the divine thousand-hooded serpent.

'Vishnudev,' he called out gently. But Vishnu was in such a deep slumber that he did not budge.

By now, Bhrigu was furious. 'At least the other two bothered to acknowledge my presence,' the sage said to himself. In a fit of anger, he kicked Vishnu on the chest to wake him up. Vishnu's wife, Lakshmi, who lived in his heart, emerged from his chest, shocked by the sudden blow.

Before she could react, she noticed that Vishnu had woken up with a start too. But instead of punishing the sage, her husband held Bhrigu's foot and began massaging it. 'Sage Bhrigu, I'm so sorry I didn't see you come in. I hope you haven't hurt your leg. Are you okay?' he said.

Enraged by Bhrigu's insult and Vishnu's meek reaction, Lakshmi decided to leave Vaikunth. Vishnu knew why his wife was upset, but he did not want to reprimand the sage either. After all, Bhrigu was one of his greatest devotees.

Bhrigu was stunned. 'If such crude behaviour does not anger you, and if you are *still* full of compassion for your devotee, then *you* are the greatest god!' he announced, and gifted Vishnu the sacred fruit from the ritual.

While Bhrigu's quest had ended, a fresh challenge had emerged for Vishnu – of finding Lakshmi. 'Now where could she have gone?' he wondered. After searching Deva Lok (the world of gods) in vain, he finally decided to head to Prithvi Lok.

With one big leap, he descended on a hill. He looked around but couldn't see Lakshmi anywhere. He took another step and reached a rocky terrain, and as he passed through the rocks that stood in his path, they instantly crumbled, making way for the greatest god. The remaining boulders, which didn't break down, formed an arch-like festoon above his head to welcome him.

'*Lakshmiiii*!' he called out, but his dear wife didn't answer. He took a third step and reached his second home, perched on a high hill, the one where he had lived after defeating Hiranyaksha. There was still no sign of Lakshmi.

Dejected, Vishnu chose to stay inside an anthill to perform penance. Years passed. One day, he heard a princess call for help. A raging elephant was charging towards her. Emerging from the anthill, the god saved her from the wild beast. Captivated by the beauty of the princess, who was named Padmavathi, Vishnu, who had now assumed a new incarnation as Venkateswara, married her. He realized that she was, in fact, an avatar or manifestation of Lakshmi.

But she wasn't *exactly* Lakshmi herself. So when the original goddess found out about the wedding, she marched to Vishnu's hilly home to confront him. 'How could you?' she asked, fuming.

'And who is *she*?' Padmavathi asked.

As both his wives stared at him questioningly, Vishnu quickly turned to stone.

Just then, Brahma rushed in to help Vishnu, and explained all that had transpired. 'This was the only way we could get Vishnu to continue living on Prithvi Lok and help mankind. But Vishnu is still devoted to you, Lakshmi! And as Venkateswara, his new form, he loves you, Padmavathi!'

'We'll watch over Prithvi Lok too then…' Padmavathi said, and Lakshmi added, '…along with the greatest god!' And with that, the two goddesses transformed themselves into stone idols as well.

Connecting the Dots...

The seven peaks of Tirumala Hills in Tirupati, Andhra Pradesh – Anjanadri, Garudadri, Narayanadri, Neeladri, Seshadri, Venkatadri and Vrushabadri – make up Vishnu's home on Prithvi Lok.

It is believed that Vishnu's footprints are embedded on Narayanadri ('Narayana's peak') where he first set foot as he descended from Vaikunth. At this sacred spot, called Srivari Paadalu ('the footprints of Vishnu'), a temple has been built. The miraculously balanced stone arch, Silathoranam, marks the place where he took his second step and walked through the rocks that broke apart to let him through. The third step brought him to Venkatadri ('Venkateswara's peak').

The stone idol that the god transformed into is worshipped at the Sri Venkateswara Temple in Tirupati.

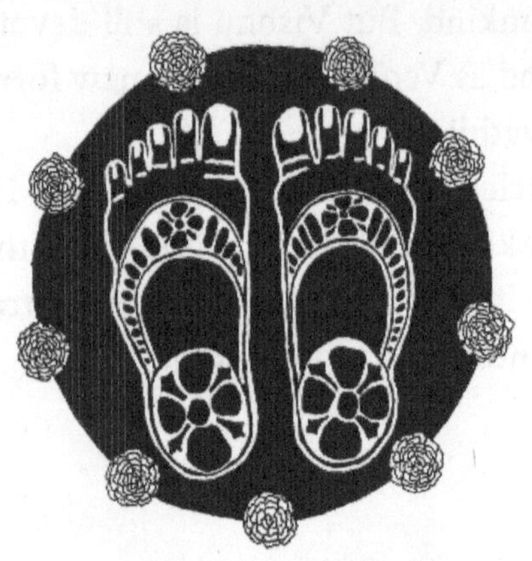

A Garland in Stone

A rare geological arch, Silathoranam is made up of a hard rock called quartzite. In Sanskrit, *sila* means 'stone' or 'rock', and *thoranam* means 'arch' as well as 'garland'. While Silathoranam resembles a floral festoon welcoming Vishnu to his second home, it is in reality a stone arch.

Silathoranam is one of the only three natural stone arches in the world, and the only one in Asia. While the rocks are said to be around 2,500 million years old, the arch is around 1,500 million years old. This means that it existed for thousands of years before the Indian plate moved away from Gondwanaland and became a peninsula. What is astonishing is that although the plate has moved (and continues to do so), the arch has stayed almost intact!

Seasonal Sculptors

So, how did the stone arch get formed in the first place? Well, it was through a process called weathering. Natural elements such as water and wind wear out or erode rocks. Weaker portions of the rocks crumble, creating large gaps in the standing rock. As more erosion takes place, the crumbled pieces of rock turn into fine soil and get blown away by the wind. Silathoranam, too, was formed in the same way.

The Geological Survey of India, which declared Silathoranam a National Geological Monument in 1981, protects it now. A fence around the rocky site makes sure that the natural arch does not get damaged.

The Perfect Frame

The rugged arch at Silathoranam is slightly higher than or almost the same height as Venkateswara's statue at the temple in Tirupati. Devotees believe that this suggests that Vishnu had indeed walked through these rocks, and the stone arch had formed over his head in the shape of a festoon. Today, a golden arch frames the lord's idol at the temple, and he is almost always depicted with a decorated festoon around him – be it in traditional paintings or in miniature figurines.

Vishnu returned to his hilly home to find Lakshmi. But did you know that there was a time when Shiva went missing and all the other gods had to go looking for him?

3

The Fiery Reflection of an Irate God

Mani Mahesh

Shiva walked on furiously. So intense was his anger that fumes began to emanate from his body. Reaching the foothills of his mountain home on Prithvi Lok, he stopped to stare at the snowy earth. Then, with a sudden flourish, he thrust his *trishul*, or trident, into the ice. It cracked, branching out like a streak of lightning, and collapsed into a large pool of cold water beneath.

He sat down on the banks of the newly formed waterbody and began meditating. But nothing could calm him down. After all, he had lost his dear wife.

Princess Sati, the daughter of King Daksha Prajapati and Queen Prasuti, was a form of Adi Shakti (the Supreme Goddess) herself. When Sati chose to marry Shiva, her father was upset. For, even though Shiva was one of the three chief gods, he did not seem very god-like. He looked unkempt, had wild, long hair, and his body was smeared with ash.

Daksha was so annoyed with Sati that when he held a sacred ceremony at his palace, he invited all his daughters and sons-in-law except Shiva. Heartbroken by her father's hurtful behaviour, Sati gave up her life. When Shiva found out about the death of his wife, he flew into a rage and was ready to destroy everything in his way. Distraught, he later took off to the only place where no one would bother him.

But Shiva was the destroyer, the slayer of demons. And so, while he was away, Taraka, a powerful asura, began terrorizing Deva Lok.

'We must find Shiva,' the gods said.

They formed search parties and looked for him in all directions.

'Can't find him in Deva Lok!'

'He is not in Patal Lok either.'

'Then he must be on Prithvi Lok!' one of them said finally. Together, they scoured the mountains that were Shiva's earthly home.

Suddenly, a light sparkling near the foothills of one caught their attention. On closer inspection, the gods realized that the light was the incandescent form of Shiva reflected in the water as he sat meditating on the lake's banks.

'Aha! Mani Mahesh!' they exclaimed, admiring Shiva's visage that shone like a sparkling jewel. Shiva had many names, and Mahesh was one of them.

'Do we wake him now?' one of them asked.

'No, his form looks serene, but he is still angry deep inside. Only Goddess Parvati can calm him now,' a god explained, and the others nodded.

Goddess Adi Shakti, who had first been born as Sati, had now reincarnated as Parvati, the daughter of Himavan and Mena, the king and queen of the Himalayas. It was now up to Parvati to bring Shiva out of his trance.

So, although the gods had found Shiva, they quietly offered their prayers to his glowing form and left him alone.

Connecting the Dots...

The lake which reflected Shiva's radiant, meditative body came to be known as Mani Mahesh Lake. This sacred waterbody is situated at the foothills of Mani Mahesh Kailash in Himachal Pradesh.

The Elusive God

The Gaddis, a tribe from Himachal Pradesh, are followers of Shiva. They believe that Shiva lives on the Mani Mahesh Kailash Peak, one of the summits that overlook the Mani Mahesh Lake. From atop the mountain, he watches over and protects their land. On most days and nights, the Mani Mahesh Kailash Peak is covered in mist and fog. When Shiva is angry and displeased, he sends avalanches and blizzards.

But when he is in a good mood, the Gaddis believe that a miracle occurs – the *mani* or jewel in his crown catches the moonlight, making the whole peak glow. The light is reflected all the way down, in the waters of Mani Mahesh Lake. Several devotees, especially those from the Gaddi tribe, visit the lake, hoping to catch a glimpse of their lord's shining jewel in the water.

The Mani Mahesh Kailash Peak is one of the five sacred Kailash peaks that make up the god's mountain abodes. The other four are Adi Kailash in Uttarakhand; Kinnaur Kailash and Shrikhand Mahadev Kailash in Himachal Pradesh; and Mount Kailash (also known as Kailash Mansarovar) in the Tibetan Himalayas.

The Runaway Bridegroom

Princess Gauri (also called Parvati) was set to marry Shiva, but she was not too pleased with the match. He was an ascetic and spent most of his time in meditation, a far cry from the charming prince she'd imagined him to be. Gauri believed that the Shiva she was going to marry was just an ordinary man, a namesake of the god. And so, she hatched a plan to disrupt her own wedding.

'What do you want for a wedding gift?' Himavan asked his daughter on the day before the wedding.

'First, promise me that you will grant whatever I ask for,' said Gauri.

'All right, I promise!' he replied.

'Great! I want you to create so much snow that the groom's party can't reach the wedding venue,' Gauri said slyly.

'But…' Himavan began, only to be reminded by his dear daughter, 'no buts, Father! You promised!'

With no choice in the matter, Himavan created such a thick blanket of snow that it was difficult for any human or god to make their way through it!

When Shiva and his wedding party reached the snow-covered mountains around Himavan's palace, he realized what was afoot.

He tapped his *trishul* on the snowy ground lightly. Out of nowhere, a herd of sheep with thick, fluffy fur emerged.

'Friends, I need your help,' Shiva said to the flock of sheep he had just created. 'My bride seems to be upset with me. Can you clear the path so that I can reach the wedding venue?' The sheep nodded, as if they had understood every word that he had said, and began walking through the snow, paving the way for the god and his companions to follow.

Soon, Shiva arrived at his destination. 'I'm here, Father-in-law,' he announced. Himavan, who was waiting at the palace gates, in the hope that his future son-in-law would somehow make it to the venue, was overjoyed. But Gauri was obviously dismayed that her grand plan had failed.

She expressed her annoyance by making arrangements for Shiva and his companions to stay in a dry, barren wood nearby.

'Princess!' her handmaiden said excitedly, rushing into her chambers. 'Your groom... You made him stay in that horrible place, but he has magically turned it into a lush, green meadow with a simple wave of his trident.'

'What?' cried Gauri.

'Yes! I also overheard one of the guests saying that your groom used his *trishul* to create some animals called "sheep", and they carved a path through the snow. He can't be an ordinary ascetic!'

'Oh!' said Gauri. She spent the rest of the evening mulling over what she had heard. 'Is he *the* great Shiva himself?' she kept asking herself. 'Yes, he must be! He turned a dry forest green. He created a new animal. And he did both using his *trishul*!' Realizing that this was indeed a match made by the gods, she decided to go ahead with the wedding.

The ceremonies began the next day. As part of the rituals, the couple had to go around the sacred fire seven times. Just as they had finished the fourth round, Shiva stopped to look at his bride. 'I'm still not sure you want to marry me,' he said.

Then, without warning, he smiled at her mischievously and began to run. Gauri froze like the snow that she had asked her father to create.

'The groom's running away! Stop him!' someone yelled.

Gauri understood that Shiva was trying to test and annoy her at the same time. She chased after him.

Shiva ran like the wind till he reached a hilly region. He then went around a lake and nimbly climbed up a mountain near it. Gauri too followed him around the lake and up the mountain.

Standing with his hands on his hips, Shiva looked at Gauri and asked, 'Oh, why have you followed me? Does this mean you *do* want to marry me?'

'Yes,' she said calmly.

The couple then went around the peak three times since they had left the sacred fire far behind. And that's how, after many twists, turns and a long trek, Shiva and Gauri finally got married!

Connecting the Dots...

This is a Gaddi myth about how the wedding of Shiva and Gauri took place. The hilly region that Shiva ran to, from his wedding venue, is called Gaderan. It is the homeland of the Gaddi tribe, who also call it Shivabhumi, or 'the land of Shiva'. The lake around which Shiva ran is the Mani Mahesh Lake, and the summit where the couple began to live after they got married is the Mani Mahesh Kailash Peak.

Following in Shiva's Footsteps

The Gaddis believe that Shiva wanted them to look after the sheep that he had created, and thus they became a shepherd community. Being ardent devotees of Shiva, the tribe's marriage customs mimic his wedding drama as well. After four circumambulations are completed in the bride's home, the groom leaves midway to become an ascetic! Later, the couple go around a pot or pan filled with water for the remaining three rounds at the groom's house to complete the rituals. The water represents the sacred Mani Mahesh Lake, which Shiva and Gauri had circled, before climbing up to Kailash.

A Luminous Peak and a Placid Lake

The glassy blue Mani Mahesh Lake, which the Mani Mahesh Kailash Peak overlooks, is a glacial lake. During the winter, a high volume of snowfall accumulates over the peak and the surrounding mountains, which are a part of the Himalayas. These turn into solid masses of ice known as glaciers. A lake formed in a region surrounded by glaciers is called a glacial lake. Some glacial lakes are created when a glacier retreats. Sometimes, avalanche debris, consisting of large sheets of ice, result in such high-altitude lakes. The Mani Mahesh Lake, however, was formed from the melting snow of the glaciers around it.

The Jewel in the Crown

The snow-clad Mani Mahesh Kailash Peak catches the rays of the moon and the sun, and casts a dazzling display of light on the lake's waters. The jewel at work here is the snow on the peak, which refracts the light that falls on it. Simply put, refraction changes the course of light and reflects it in another direction.

This miraculous event occurs only on certain days, when the moon or the sun casts its light on the peak from a specific angle, such that it travels in a particular direction and is reflected by the lake. Believing this to be the handiwork of Shiva, devotees consider such days sacred. They bathe in the lake and wait to see the glowing light, a phenomenon they call *mani darshan*.

But it may not be long before this jewel stops spreading its magical light. The Mani Mahesh Glacier recedes by 29–30 metres every year due to climate change. The degradation of the region can lead to disasters such as avalanches. And that might just mean that Shiva is angry...*very angry*.

The Search for a New Land

While the gods preferred to reside on mountains, early humans have always chosen to live next to waterbodies. But water, life-giving as it may be, is also a creature of change, which can manifest in many ways – from a deluge and a drought, to even a demon that draws power from water! – forcing entire settlements to flee and find new homes.

Thankfully, humans have got by with a little bit of help – from gods, sages and even wild animals willing to share space with them…

4

The Cradle of Human Civilization

Kullu

What do I do? Shraddhadeva thought, his face white. The boat rocked dangerously as the waves grew more turbulent. The strong gusts of wind didn't help either. The sages were trying to stay calm, focusing on their sacred chants. But the animals on board were feeling agitated and seasick.

Shraddhadeva dropped to his knees, raised his hands skywards and called out to some unseen force, 'Help me… Take us to safety!'

As if in response to his plea, there was a blinding flash – the colour of bright moonlight – that caused the boat to rock even more wildly. Then, there was a big splash…

King Shraddhadeva Manu ruled over a vast oceanside kingdom. He loved acquiring knowledge and often enjoyed long conversations with learned sages. He was a kind king, and showed compassion towards humans and animals alike. Little did he know that his life would soon take an unexpected turn.

It all began on the day he stopped by a river to quench his thirst. As he cupped some of the clean water in his palms, he noticed a tiny, silvery white fish inside them.

'Help me! Please take me to safety!' the fish squeaked. Although the king was taken aback, he didn't throw the talking fish back into the river.

'A big fish is chasing me! It wants to eat me up!' the little fish said.

Shraddhadeva carefully transferred the fish, along with some water, into a pot and took it home. The fish was no ordinary being, he realized. Not only could it talk, but it also grew in size rapidly with each passing day. From the water pot, he shifted the fish to a bigger clay pot, and then to a larger cooking vessel. When the fish outgrew that, he placed it in a large pond in his palace garden. But the fish just kept growing. And as it grew, Shraddhadeva noticed a horn starting to jut out of its head.

Finally, when Shraddhadeva didn't have a suitable waterbody left to shift the growing fish into, he had it transported to the ocean that surrounded his kingdom.

'Be free, my friend. Grow as much as you want,' Shraddhadeva said as he bid the fish goodbye.

'I'll repay your kindness someday, Manu,' the horned fish replied. 'A great flood is about to strike the earth. I'm afraid everything will perish.'

'How do you know that?' Shraddhadeva asked.

A bright light appeared, and the top half of the fish transformed to reveal its true divine form, while the lower half remained the same.

'Vishnu!' Shraddhadeva exclaimed, bowing reverently.

'Rise, Manu. I had to appear in my Matsya avatar to make sure the world continues to exist. In you, I see a worthy saviour!' Vishnu said. 'Build a large boat – and gather nine kinds of grain and every species of wildlife on it.'

'*W-wildlife?*' Shraddhadeva asked, looking extremely worried.

'Yes, one male and one female from every species,' Matsya explained. 'Most importantly, knowledge must survive. So, protect the seven chief sages, who will continue to guide mankind on Prithvi Lok. Hurry, you don't have much time! And trust me, you can do this.'

Without wasting a single minute, Shraddhadeva followed every instruction that Matsya had given him. By the time he had rounded up all the wild creatures, collected the grains, convinced the seven sages to join him and finished constructing a sturdy boat, dark, menacing clouds had begun to appear on the horizon.

'I have never seen anything like this before,' Shraddhadeva said to himself. Making sure that the sages as well as the animals were aboard, he began steering the boat. It started raining heavily, and soon enough, a great flood occurred. Like Matsya had foretold, it washed away everything and everyone.

As he travelled far into the ocean, Shraddhadeva knew that his entire kingdom was lost. The boat rocked dangerously; he realized that he could no longer manoeuvre it over the turbulent waves. In desperation, he fell to his knees and hoped divine forces would help him.

That's when the ball of white light, which had appeared out of nowhere, dived into the water with such force that the boat shook again. As Shraddhadeva steadied himself to see what had caused the splash, he saw a familiar form. It was the silvery white fish!

'Great job, Manu!' Matsya called out.

'Thanks, but I don't think we'll make it,' the king said sadly.

'I'm here now,' said the giant fish reassuringly.

On Matsya's instructions, Shraddhadeva threw a looped rope around its horn (which had grown even bigger!), and the fish swam through the rough waters, expertly pulling the boat along. The floodwaters seemed never-ending. At long last, when a few pointed peaks were visible in the distance, Matsya yelled, 'Hold on! We're almost there.'

As Shraddhadeva and the seven sages clutched the boat's wooden flank, the fish jumped out of the water, soared into the air and landed on a high mountain peak. So great was its strength that the boat too landed with a gentle thud behind it.

The water levels kept rising, but the peak was high enough. Shraddhadeva couldn't believe that they had actually managed to survive the great deluge.

'Thank you for trusting me with this task,' he said to the giant fish.

'When the waters recede, begin a fresh life, a new civilization in the valley below,' Matsya said, before disappearing into the raging waters.

Long after the flood had retreated, Shraddhadeva and the sages built a new settlement in the valley. He released the wildlife into the surrounding forests and hills so that they could choose their own territories. He sowed the seeds he had brought with him and was relieved when the land began to thrive with greenery, and food began to grow.

Now that Shraddhadeva had fulfilled his duty, he began feeling lonely in the unfamiliar region. He

enjoyed his conversations with the seven sages but missed his family and friends. So, one day, he prayed to a river flowing nearby for a companion he could share his life with. Lo and behold, a lady emerged from the waters! Soon enough, with the blessings of the sages, they got married, and together, they started the first human family after the great deluge. Shraddhadeva's children came to be known as *manava*, a word that is used to collectively refer to human beings today.

Connecting the Dots...

Legend has it that Vishnu, as Matsya, had taken the boat to the top of a Himalayan peak in the Kullu Valley in Himachal Pradesh. The word Kullu possibly has its roots in the ancient kingdom of Kuluta, which was situated in this region more than two millennia ago. Another theory suggests that it came from an earlier name, Kulanta Pitha, or 'the last habitable world'. This is perhaps why Matsya brought the king's boat here during the flood. The exact place where Shraddhadeva Manu settled was earlier called Manu Aalaya ('Manu's abode'). Over time, its name was shortened to Manali, a picturesque hill station in present-day Himachal Pradesh.

The Sunken Continent

Shraddhadeva Manu's kingdom is said to have been in Kumari Kandam, a landmass as big as a continent, attached to the southern end of ancient India. It is believed that the land, along with his kingdom, sank into the Indian Ocean after being hit by a tsunami. Some experts have tried to establish that Kumari Kandam was, in fact, Lemuria (an antique land also believed to have submerged in the Indian Ocean after a tsunami). Others suggest that they were two different lands as Lemuria was located where Indonesia is now. A third group has refuted these two theories – they believe that both Kumari Kandam and Lemuria are mythical places!

Wild Runs the Water

While Kumari Kandam and Lemuria may or may not have been drowned by a tsunami, Kullu Valley in Himachal Pradesh is regularly ravaged by floods even today. Valleys are usually formed by flowing rivers and running rainwater. Over the course of several years, the flowing water erodes the earth's surface, creating cracks or crevices. It also erodes rocks and boulders from surrounding mountains and glaciers. Thus, a low or sloping area of land – a valley – is formed between mountains.

Sitting on the banks of the Beas River, in the lap of the Pir Panjal and the Greater Himalayan ranges, Kullu is affected by the monsoon winds as well as the freezing and melting of the glaciers in the region. So, it is prone to rainstorms and flash floods, which bring down a large volume of eroded sediment and often destroy homes, towns and human lives.

The Great Flood

Most mythologies from around the world tell stories of how mighty deities caused a major flood to begin a new cycle of life in the world and chose a single human hero for this task.

According to Indian mythology, Shraddhadeva Manu is that saviour. In Greek mythology, it is Deucalion, while ancient Mesopotamia has a similar hero in Gilgamesh. The Bible talks about the flood and the repopulation of the world in the tale of Noah and his ark.

These stories are possibly based on somewhat true events – many civilizations across the world have indeed faced devastating floods, most probably caused by unexpected, heavy rainfall. In such a case, as a huge amount of water suddenly collects on land, it is not easily absorbed by the earth. It then takes a while for the waters to recede.

Some geologists suggest that the great flood mentioned in the Shraddhadeva story was caused by a comet which struck the Indian Ocean! This, in turn, gave rise to a tsunami that flooded and washed away much of the land and its inhabitants.

From Whither Cometh the Comet

The word comet comes from the Greek word *kometes*, which denotes a 'long-haired star'. Since comets usually have a tail of pearly white light, people in olden times thought they were stars with hair! Some mythologies even suggest that comets have a horn. Depending on its position around the sun and the surrounding solar winds, a comet's tail may sometimes appear in front of it. This may make it look like the comet has a horn. Isn't it strange then that the giant, silvery white fish that told Shraddhadeva about the impending flood also had a horn on its head?

Kullu became home to a different race of humans after the floodwaters receded on their own. But did you know that a divine being was forced to drain a waterbody and create a new valley once?

5

Where a Water Monster Once Lived

Kashmir

'I told you! This isn't going anywhere,' Nila exclaimed, looking hopelessly at Sage Kashyapa.

'Well, there's only one way then,' said the sage, turning to Vishnu.

Vishnu nodded and let out a big sigh.

'All right, Jalodbhava, let's play a game,' the blue-skinned god said.

But the water monster only yawned in response.

'Can you escape my *sudarshan chakra*?' Vishnu asked as he swiftly released his trademark weapon – a spinning disc with serrated edges – towards Jalodbhava.

'Yeah,' Jalodbhava drawled, lazily dodging the spinning disc that missed him by a whisker.

'He is still in the water. Even if he hadn't dodged it, the *sudarshan chakra* couldn't have harmed him,' Nila muttered softly to Kashyapa. The sage shushed him.

'Hmm... Can you match my size then?' Vishnu asked, as his form grew bigger and bigger, making the mountains around him look like miniatures.

'I can't believe I am missing my nap for this silly game!' the monster said, instantly matching Vishnu in height and size.

'But can you look this fierce?' Vishnu roared, transforming into a ferocious animal. With red, beady eyes flashing his rage and two long, pointed tusks glistening in the sunlight, he was now Varaha, the giant wild boar.

Nila and the Naga people, who had been watching from the sidelines, stepped back. They definitely didn't want to be in the way of this avatar of Vishnu!

But Jalodbhava only rolled his eyes and sneered, 'Oh, what a bore!'

Set in the midst of tall, snow-capped mountains, Satisar was a beautiful lake named after Goddess Sati. But much to everyone's dismay, an evil monster called Jalodbhava came to live in this lake one day.

For centuries, the Naga people, who were semi-human and semi-serpentine in form, had lived in the region surrounding the lake. But ever since Jalodbhava had invaded the lake, they were terrified of approaching it, even for their basic water needs.

'I am Jalodbhava, "the one who was born from water". And you are all, basically, my food,' he declared. This wasn't an empty threat, as the monster did eat up anyone who approached the banks of the lake.

Nila, the king of the Nagas, was the son of Sage Kashyapa. Unable to bear Jalodbhava's atrocities any longer, he sought his father's help. 'The other day, a child strayed towards the banks while playing with her friends. But before any of us could warn her, Jalodbhava emerged out of the water and…' Nila trailed off, his voice quavering. 'We don't know what to do, Father!'

'Why, you're the king, Nila. You can't give up. You must fight him!' Kashyapa responded matter-of-factly.

'Yes, I *know* that, but Jalodbhava is a *water* monster – he cannot be defeated as long as he is in the water. And of course, he *never* leaves the lake,' Nila explained.

Kashyapa thought for a bit and said, 'This is a job for Vishnu then.'

And so, he sent out a request to Vishnu, who arrived immediately. The Nagas gathered to see how the god would free the lake of the monster.

'Jalodbhava!' Vishnu yelled.

'Who's disturbing my slumber? *Yawn.* Ah, the great Vishnu himself has come to see me! I can't believe my eyes,' Jalodbhava said, rubbing his eyes for effect.

'I'm not here to see you, I'm here to fight you!'

'*Tsk tsk tsk...* I knew these squiggly Nagas would tell on me. But you know what, you picked the wrong day. I've just gobbled up a few fat, juicy Nagas. Can't move too much,' Jalodbhava groaned, moving heavily from side to side.

'Don't worry, Jalodbhava! Once I defeat you, you won't be able to move at all!' Vishnu said.

'I see! Since you've made up your mind to fight me, why don't you come into the water? I'm known for my hospitality,' the water monster said with a wicked grin.

'This isn't going anywhere,' Nila muttered to his father, as they watched the game of one-upmanship between them.

But the sage was sure that Vishnu had some unexpected move up his sleeve. And he did!

The god suddenly transformed himself into the grunting Varaha.

Everyone was taken aback, but not Jalodbhava. 'Come on, you bore, fight me!' he said. Varaha stomped his feet and dug the earth with them, making the mud fly in every direction. As the Nagas watched, the wild boar began to charge, but instead of rushing towards the water monster, he headed straight towards the huge mountains in the distance. Whacking them hard with his tusks and butting them with his head, Varaha made a huge hole in one of them.

'I knew he had a plan!' Kashyapa said to his son.

'Wonderful!' Nila exclaimed. He knew exactly what Varaha was trying to do.

The waters of Satisar began gushing out through the gaping hole in the mountains.

'Hey, wait! What's going on here?' yelled Jalodbhava.

Soon, the lake was completely drained. The shocked and confused Jalodbhava was now surrounded by a sludgy lakebed. The monster's protection was gone! A massive battle then took place between Varaha and Jalodbhava, in which the monster was finally defeated.

As Nila and the Nagas thanked Vishnu, Kashyapa stood on the lake's mucky banks, lost in contemplation.

'What if my people and I settle here someday?' the sage asked, pointing to the vast lakebed. 'Would you mind that, Nila?'

The Naga king thought for a bit, since Sage Kashyapa lived among humans, most of whom were fellow sages and his disciples. Nila knew that agreeing to his father's request meant that the Nagas would now have to share the land with humans. He decided to ask the Naga people instead. 'Would *you* mind?'

Not all of them were comfortable with this idea, but one of the Nagas, who didn't have a problem with this arrangement, said, 'How can we mind? If it weren't for Sage Kashyapa, Vishnu wouldn't have come here to free us from Jalodbhava's terror.'

'That's right,' some other Nagas chorused.

'It's decided then,' Vishnu said to the sage. 'Someday, this will be one of the greenest and lushest valleys in the country. Go ahead and make it your home, Kashyapa.'

Over time, when the lakebed became habitable, Kashyapa and his people made it their home. That is how humans and the Naga people came to live together in this mountainous region.

Connecting the Dots...

The fertile land that was formed by the draining of the Satisar Lake is the Kashmir Valley. Some say that its name comes from the term Kashyapa Mar, which means 'abode of Kashyapa'. Others believe that the word Kashmir is a combination of ka *('water') and* shimeera *('desiccated' or 'dried out'), thus meaning the 'land formed by desiccating a waterbody'. The place where Varaha punctured a hole in the mountains came to be called Varahamula. A city in present-day Kashmir, it is now known as Baramulla.*

Another version of the Jalodbhava story suggests that it was Sage Kashyapa, not Vishnu, who drained the lake, fought and defeated Jalodbhava, and created Kashmir. However, according to a Tibetan Buddhist legend, the valley was created when a monk called Madhyantika outwitted a dragon who lived in the lake and convinced the creature to drain its waters completely.

The Wrath of Zoji La

A fascinating Tibetan Buddhist tale narrates how Ladakh (previously a part of Kashmir, now a union territory) became a barren region, and how the high mountain pass called Zoji La, which connects Kashmir to Ladakh, was formed. Once, Naropa, the husband of Du-zhi Lhamo, the goddess of the four seasons in this land, refused to let her accompany him on a journey to Ladakh. The upset goddess turned herself into a mountain pass that separated Kashmir from Ladakh, making sure that her back was turned towards Ladakh while she faced her homeland, Kashmir. Since she was the goddess of the four seasons, Kashmir remained green and fertile on her watch. Ladakh, on the other hand, could not enjoy the gifts of nature and turned into a desert.

The mountain pass of Du-zhi Lhamo is now called Zoji La; in the Tibetan language, spoken widely in Ladakh, it means the 'pass of the blizzards'. True to its name, it is counted among the most dangerous roads in the world today. An extremely narrow pass, high walls of snow run alongside it for much of its length. Perhaps it is the goddess's anger that still manifests as the blizzards and avalanches unleashed on travellers on this route.

A Fertile Treasure

The Satisar Lake is also known as Karewa Lake. The valley of Kashmir, which has taken the lake's place, is known for its *karewas*. These are unique land formations that lie between the Greater Himalayas (the highest part of the Himalayas) and the Pir Panjal Range (which runs through Himachal Pradesh and Jammu and Kashmir).

In Kashmiri, *karewa* means 'raised plateau'. It is, essentially, a lakebed – several thousand feet in height – made up of clay and silt deposits. The raised silt plateaux were formed through two processes – the draining of the Karewa Lake and the activity of the surrounding glaciers.

The soil of the *karewas* is suitable for growing almonds, apples, apricots, maize, walnuts and especially saffron (*zaffran* in the Kashmiri language). However, these orchards and farms are slowly declining today, due to the rampant extraction of the *karewas* soil for use as landfill and in the construction of new railway lines and roads. The loss of the *karewas* will not only affect agriculture, but also increase the risk of earthquakes in this already seismically active region.

Making Way for the Valley

Many millennia ago, the Tethys Sea, an expansive waterbody, separated the ancient landmasses of Laurasia and Gondwanaland. After the Indian plate collided with the Eurasian plate, the space occupied by the Tethys was eventually closed. Today, the Indian Ocean, India and some other countries in South Asia are situated where the sea existed.

Geologists propose that before the Indian plate joined the Eurasian plate, Kashmir was under the Tethys. After that collision, the Zanskar Range in the Greater Himalayas and the Pir Panjal Range in the Lesser (or Lower) Himalayas formed in that region.

As proof of the fact that parts of Kashmir and Ladakh were once underwater, scientists have found the impressions of waves and marine fossils across these mountains. Even a hippopotamus's skull was found in Ladakh in 1992. Studies also suggest that the rocks on the peaks of Zanskar were actually formed many kilometres beneath the earth's surface and then thrown up to this height through tectonic activity.

As the Indian plate continues to move and bend below the Eurasian plate, it has caused pressure or stress to the Himalayan land. An earthquake usually occurs to release such built-up pressure. Geologists are constantly studying the landscape to predict when the next big quake might shake up the Himalayas.

Meanwhile, after the formation of these ranges, a high volume of snowfall accumulated over these mountains during the winter and turned into glaciers. Slowly, the glaciers began melting and became the source of many rivers, and brought down large deposits of rock, sediment and ice into the valleys below. Here, the ice melted further and formed into lakes.

The Karewa Lake, one such waterbody, was created between Zanskar and Pir Panjal. An earthquake caused a portion of the mountains in Baramulla to break apart, creating a gap for the waters of Karewa Lake to drain out. The land that emerged thereafter, consisted of *karewas*, formed by glacial and lake deposits. This became the Kashmir Valley.

A Desert in the Mountains

Ladakh is a cold desert. Such deserts are typically found in high altitudes. The climate here is icy cold in the winter.

The Himalayan range does not let rain clouds pass into Ladakh, making it a rain shadow region. This is why Ladakh is largely barren, while Kashmir is green and fertile. Looks like Goddess Du-zhi Lhamo, as Zoji La, indeed controls the seasons here!

Humans came to live in the Kashmir Valley after Satisar had been drained. But did you know that an entire community of people had to find new homes because the river they lived next to mysteriously went underground?

6

Rising from the Sea

Benaulim

'Forgive me, Parashurama! But I cannot obey you. The waters will stay where they are!' Varuna said.

'Think it over, Varuna,' Parashurama said calmly.

Everyone knew of Parashurama's infamous wrath, including Varuna. Yet, he replied, 'I'm sure, Parashurama. I don't need to think about it again. I cannot and will not move the waters.'

'I see!' Parashurama said, his eyes narrowing. 'Then I shall do as I please.'

Rama, the warrior-sage and son of Sage Jamdagni, stood on a cliff that overlooked a vast sea. He was tired. He had waged many battles against warriors he thought were corrupt and unjust. As the son of a sage, Rama wasn't meant to take up arms. But he had. The *parashu*, or axe, had become an indispensable part of his being, even giving him the name 'Parashurama'.

His whole life played out as a reel of memories as he stood gazing at the sea. He had been an obedient son to his father, from whom he knew he had received the legacy of rage. So, when Sage Jamdagni was killed by a powerful king, Kartavirya Arjuna, Parashurama's rage could not be contained. What had begun as a quest for revenge against his father's murderer went on to become a long fight against entire clans of warriors.

The sea breeze fell on his dishevelled hair and beard and brought him back to the present.

'This feels like home,' Parashurama muttered.

As the rose-orange sky reflected in his eyes, the warrior-sage called upon Varuna, the god of oceans and seas. 'O Varuna, move your waters inwards, and create a mass of land where I can stay and perform a yajna.'

Varuna appeared and politely refused. 'Parashurama, I'm happy this land gives you peace. But I can't move the waters. Please settle on the land that is already visible.'

'I wish to perform the yajna on a new piece of land. I know of families from the northern and western regions who are homeless at the moment. The river they lived along has vanished. They have been living here and there temporarily but are now looking for a permanent place near a waterbody. If you make the sea recede just a bit, they can come and settle here,' Parashurama explained.

But Varuna refused to budge.

Furious, Parashurama shot an arrow far into the sea.

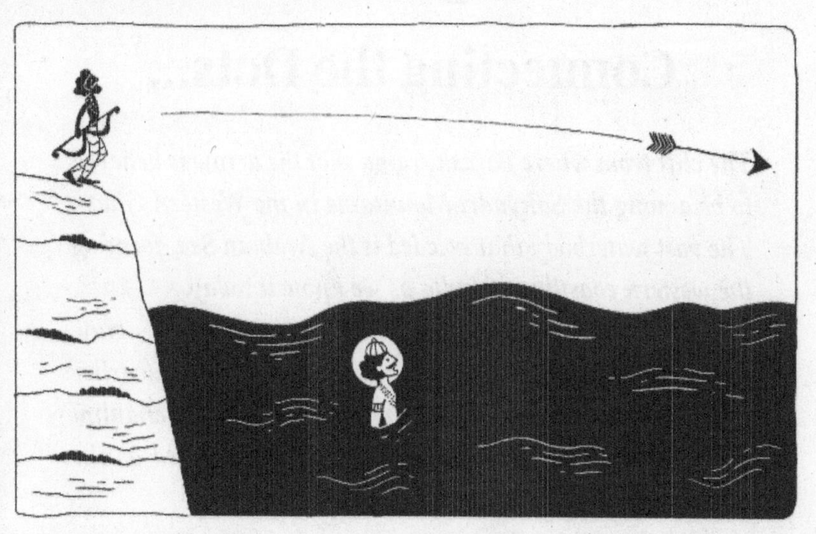

The waters immediately retreated to the very spot where the arrow had struck the seabed. An additional strip of land, somewhat like a beach, appeared along the coast. As the waters kept receding further down the entire stretch of the sea, more land emerged. And a whole coastline was formed!

Much as he tried, Varuna could not get the waters to move ahead of the arrow and back to their original position. Upset and helpless, he retreated into the sea.

Having defeated Varuna without so much as a fight, Parashurama invited the homeless families to conduct a yajna on the freshly formed land and settle there.

'After a long time,' Parashurama said to himself, 'I think I've done a good deed.'

Connecting the Dots...

The cliff from where Parashurama shot the arrow is believed to be among the Sahyadri Mountains in the Western Ghats. The vast waterbody that receded is the Arabian Sea, forming the western coastline of India as we know it today.

The beach that emerged when Parashurama's arrow struck the seabed is known now as Benaulim Beach (earlier called Banahalli, meaning 'village of the arrow'). Benaulim is in present-day Goa, the region that was formed as the land rose along the coast.

The Disciples of Saraswat

The families to whom Parashurama gifted the coastal land are known as Saraswat Brahmins. The people of this community are originally believed to have lived along the banks of River Saraswati, where they learnt the Vedas from Saraswat, the river's son. But when the river dried up (some say it went underground), they were forced to move and settle along the western coast of India.

Waves and the Waterfront

Thousands of years ago – some say, as far back as 10,000 BCE – major movements in the tectonic plates around the western coast of the Indian subcontinent caused a huge mass of submerged land to rise above the sea.

Extending inwards, from the Arabian Sea to the Western Ghats, this raised land runs along the western fringes of Maharashtra and Goa as Konkan, Karnataka as Kanara, and Kerala as the Malabar Coast. This long coastline consists of hills, plateaux, plains, and most importantly, a number of beautiful beaches! Goa, which was formed with the creation of this coastline, is known as the land of beaches.

A beach is formed at the edge of a sea or ocean, when the waves deposit sand, rocks or pebbles along the coastline over hundreds of years. When rocks and minerals break down into fine particles, they form sand. The colour of sand on a beach thus depends on the rock or mineral it comes from. Not just minerals, but waves often wash ashore all kinds of marine organisms – from molluscs and their shells, anemones and seaweed to sharks and whales.

The waves also return the tonnes of plastic waste that humans discard into the oceans.

Goa Rocks!

Having formed over many millennia, the terrain of Goa is made up of several kinds of rocks. Huge, grey rocks sit on the shores of Palolem Beach. Called trondhjemite gneisses, these are rocks that existed way before the supercontinent Pangaea was even formed. The ones found in Goa are around 3.4 billion years old!

The Saraswat Brahmins were relieved to find a home in this region. But did you know that Parashurama had to solve a strange problem faced by the families who went to settle in the southernmost area of this coastal belt?

7

Under the Serpent's Gaze

Sarpa Kaavu

'Sage Parashurama, we can't build houses in the new territory you gave us,' an elderly man said, wiping the sweat on his brow. He hadn't come alone – many of the families rendered homeless by the Saraswati's disappearance stood behind him.

Confused, the warrior-sage asked, 'Why not? That land is near the coast. It is lush and fertile. What more could you ask for?'

'No, no, all that is fine,' the elderly man said, fidgeting with his sash. 'But there's a problem... It's infested with snakes!'

'Snakes?' Parashurama repeated.

'Yes, venomous ones. Hundreds...no, *thousands* of them!' the man said, the terror clearly visible in his eyes.

Parashurama had gifted some of the new coastal land he had created to other Saraswat Brahmin families who were still looking for a place to settle in. However, after they told him about the presence of snakes there, Parashurama visited the region to see if he could find a solution.

'Oh my!' he exclaimed when he got to the place.

There truly were thousands of venomous snakes, especially cobras, wriggling everywhere.

'O powerful Shiva, the one who wears a serpent around his neck, help us!' Parashurama called out and sat down (away from the snakes) to perform penance.

When Shiva appeared, he told the warrior-sage, 'Parashurama, this is the abode of the serpents. I can't and won't make them leave this place.'

'I'm sorry, I didn't know. But how can I tell these families that they can't live here now? Where will they go?'

'Hmm…' said Shiva, mulling it over. He didn't have the heart to turn away the homeless families either. 'All right, if humans want to live here, they will have to request the snakes to give them some space.'

'You mean, *pray* to them?' Parashurama asked.

'Yes, offer prayers to the great serpent king, Vasuki. Only the snakes can help you. It is their land, after all.'

Once again, Parashurama prayed so fervently that Vasuki appeared before him. The head and torso of the serpent king were just like a human's. But instead of legs, he had a long, coiled snake tail. And over his human-like head, were his five hooded snake heads.

Towering over Parashurama and the region's thick, tall trees, Vasuki looked majestic. 'What is it that you wish, O wise sage?' he asked.

'O generous Vasuki, I have promised this land to these homeless people. But I did not know then that it belonged to you. Shiva says that only you have the right to decide if humans can live here with all of you.'

'That's right,' Vasuki hissed.

'If you and your serpents could give these families some space to make their homes, I'd be so grateful,' Parashurama said with folded hands.

'Hmm, humans?' Vasuki narrowed his beady serpent eyes and studied the people who stood trembling behind Parashurama. 'I'm not too sure I trust them,' he said slowly, lowering his gigantic hoods to take a closer look at them. Some of them screamed. The elderly man fainted.

'They lead a simple life,' Parashurama said. 'They will never harm any of your kind.'

'I want to believe you, Parashurama, but...'

There was complete silence. No one stirred, not even the snakes. They wanted to know what their king would decide. Vasuki then looked at all the serpents. One by one, thousands of them raised their hoods, as though they were acknowledging what their king had said. Not a word was exchanged, nor a hiss, not even a swish of the tail. Vasuki waited till each and every hood was up, as if he wanted their consensus. When the last serpent had raised its hood, Vasuki spoke. 'It's decided then,' he told Parashurama. 'We will let them stay on our land.'

'Thank you –' Parashurama began, but Vasuki interrupted him. 'There are a few conditions! Every family must create sacred groves for my serpents around their homes. They must worship us forever. Nothing, and I mean *nothing*, will ever be taken from our groves, not even a dried flower.'

'Whatever you say,' Parashurama readily agreed.

'Tell your humans to never forget our kindnes. Never forget that we serpents are and will always be the guardians of this land!'

Parashurama gestured to the people who stood around him, and they bowed to Vasuki to show him that they had agreed to all his terms.

'I'll be watching,' Vasuki told the people, his eyes gleaming. With that, the serpent king disappeared.

The serpents gave the humans space to begin building their homes on their land. As promised, the families made sure that they kept a sacred forest-like space around their homes. Parashurama dug the earth with his axe and installed the first set of stone idols of Vasuki and other snake gods and goddesses, to make sure the families would worship them regularly. Ever since, humans and snakes have resided together in this verdant land.

Connecting the Dots...

The coastal stretch mentioned in this tale is the Malabar Coast in Kerala. The sacred serpent groves, which Vasuki asked the settlers to build, have been an essential part of traditional homes in the state for centuries. In Malayalam, these groves are called sarpa kaavu – sarpa *means 'serpent' and* kaavu *refers to the 'grove with the shrine'.*

Guardians of the Divine Forests

All over the world, groups of people or certain communities get together to protect small forests in their neighbourhoods. These are known as sacred groves as they are usually dedicated to a local deity or forest spirit. To mark them as holy, people from the community install idols of such deities, creating a mini shrine inside the area. They become the guardians of the groves.

Worshipping the idols regularly is a way to make sure that humans remember to follow the rules of the forest. They are not supposed to pluck flowers or fruits, cut trees, harm the wildlife or disturb the peace of the groves. Although beliefs vary across communities, a common notion is that anyone who disobeys these rules will be punished by the divine guardians.

Rite at the Altar

People worship the idols of Naga Raja, Naga Kanya, Naga Yakshi and other Naga *devatas* in the *sarpa kaavu* that dot Kerala. Every evening, they light lamps in front of the idols. On special days, rituals such as Theyyam (a folk dance in which tales of snakes and serpent deities, along with many others, are performed), Sarpam Paattu (songs dedicated to serpents) and Sarpa Kalam (drawings of snake deities made on the ground with coloured powders) are also practised at the sacred groves.

Of Entwined Trees and Serpentine Streams

The practice of considering such groves sacred also helps conserve natural ecosystems. Several species of wildlife, which cannot be easily spotted elsewhere, have been found in these groves by ecologists. Many rare medicinal plants have been discovered too, and preserved in these forest sanctuaries.

Sacred groves can be big or small. They are natural forests, which means that humans take care of them, but they do not usually plant trees within these spaces.

The trees and wildlife found in them depend on various factors, such as the type of soil, climate and the availability of water.

Every element in these groves helps preserve the ecological balance of the place and minimize pollution. The roots of trees hold the soil together, protecting the land from erosion and floods. Dried leaves and animal waste decay and become a part of the soil, adding nutrients to it. The groves also act as rainwater reservoirs, and often have streams or ponds within their precincts. This is how they provide groundwater to the wildlife as well as the human settlements around them.

In the legend of Parashurama and the snakes, the Saraswat Brahmins had to migrate after the waters of River Saraswati dried up. So, it is possible that Parashurama chose this area, with its thick forests and streams, as their new home, because both he and the families knew the importance of living close to waterbodies.

The Blurry Divide

Generations of families from different communities have been taking care of sacred groves across India, especially the *sarpa kaavu* of Kerala. However, these days, people have begun finding new ways to flout the rules of these forests. They shift the idols to another place in the grove (sometimes, outside it), so that they can cut trees in the area or even destroy entire groves to make way for buildings, hotels, roads and bridges.

As more and more groves are cleared, snakes are often forced to leave their natural habitats, leading to snake-human conflict. Either serpents get killed by humans, or humans are bitten by venomous snakes. This is probably why Vasuki and the serpents laid down the rules, all that time ago, knowing fully well that someday, humans would forget their kindness and the fact that the serpents are the original guardians of these groves.

The Powers That Preserve

Humans have not always been the best protectors of the natural world. So, that responsibility has largely fallen on the shoulders of the divine beings – in Hindu mythology, it rests with Vishnu and his various avatars.

The preserver, as he is called, shares a strange equation with geographical elements, some of which are curiously endowed with the ability to think and act like the divine protector himself...

8

The Black Waters

Yamuna

A shining river flowed through Braj, passing through several villages along its course. Vrindavan, where little Krishna lived, was one of them. He spent all his free time (and he had a lot of it at his age!) on the banks of the river.

One day, as Krishna and his friends were playing a game of catch, their ball rolled into the river. Krishna stood at the edge of the bank, staring into the glimmering water. Then, he turned to look at his friends and smiled mischievously. Before they could read his mind, he jumped straight into the river.

Vrindavan, a quaint village in the land of Braj, was home to the Yadava people, a community of cattle herders. Ever since the Yadava chief's family had seen an addition in the form of little Krishna, a lot had changed in the village.

In no time, Krishna had become the darling of Vrindavan. With his cute antics and naughty pranks, the boy kept his mother, Yashoda, and the entire village on their toes. He would throw pebbles at the earthen pots that milkmaids carried on their heads. He would steal and gorge on butter, his favourite snack. He would hide and refuse to come out for hours, even when he could see that Yashoda was looking for him frantically. Yet, whatever Krishna did, the people of Vrindavan found him so endearing that they could never truly be angry with him. There was magic in the way he played the flute, and its lilting notes filled everyone with happiness and peace.

Of course, there was another reason for Krishna's popularity. He was no ordinary child – he had divine powers, which people witnessed first-hand every time he fought a demon or monster who came to kill him. No, it wasn't normal for the Yadavas to have these frightening creatures saunter into their lives and lanes – in fact, when an increasing number of demons began visiting their original homeland, Gokul, the community had moved to Vrindavan overnight to keep the children safe. But Vrindavan too became the centre of such visits. The latest visitor seemed to have a larger plan – to destroy all of Vrindavan and its beings, not just Krishna.

The inhabitants of the village had been keeping away from the river because its sparkling blue waters had mysteriously turned into a murky black.

At first, no one could understand why their dear river had changed so. But one day, some inhabitants saw a few dark hoods rise out of its waters. Kaliya, a many-headed venomous snake, had made the river his home, along with his large family. His venom had spread through the water, turning it black.

'I'll teach that Kaliya a lesson,' little Krishna fumed.

'No, you won't!' said Yashoda, glaring at him. 'No going near the river! Got it?'

Krishna gave her a reluctant half-nod.

'Did you hear what I said?' she asked again.

'*Okayyyy*!' he said, playfully jumping into her lap and hugging her.

But that day, when the ball rolled into the river, Krishna did exactly what he had been forbidden to do.

A group of milkmaids who were passing by the river asked the children what had happened.

'Krishna...*gulp*...jumped into the river...' they said, amidst frightened sobs. 'Kaliya won't eat him up, will he?'

As the milkmaids looked at each other in shock, one of the children ran to Krishna's house and yelled, 'Yashoda Ma, your Krishna has dived into the river to fetch a ball!'

Yashoda sprinted to the river, and paced up and down its banks, anxiously calling out, '*Krishnaaa! Krishnaaaaa*!'

But there was no response.

Meanwhile, deep under the water, little Krishna had found the ball. But he was more interested in the thick, long, black tail that he had spotted on the riverbed. He tugged at it.

'Who dares touch Kaliya's tail?' the giant snake called out, as his many heads came hissing towards Krishna. (The snake always referred to himself in the third person. It made him feel important!)

'Hello, I'm Krishna. I want to play with your tail,' the boy replied.

'Not allowed! Now leave, before your mother never finds you,' Kaliya snarled.

'Okay, let me dance on your head then, *pleeaase?*' Krishna teased.

'Don't you want to live, boy?' Kaliya said menacingly, coming closer to the child. 'You should be afraid of Kaliya. If Kaliya catches you –'

'Oh yes, that's a nice game,' Krishna interrupted. 'I'll run, and you catch me, *okayyy?*' The boy giggled and began running around.

'What? No! Kaliya does not play games. Kaliya only crushes little children with the venom in his fearsome fangs,' the snake said, revealing his large, pointed teeth.

But Krishna paid no heed. He began a game of dodge and escape with the snake. He hopped around Kaliya's tail, walked over his body, and went round and round too.

'Wait, Kaliya will get you! No, don't you dare touch Kaliya's tail... Stop! Tickling is not allowed... Now, you're making Kaliya angry. *Hissss!*' The snake darted around but was unable to match the boy's speed.

Hearing all the commotion, the other snakes in Kaliya's family came to see what the matter was. They were horrified to find the mighty Kaliya looking so helpless in front of a playful human child. So, they joined Kaliya in his attempts to catch Krishna.

'*Nooo*, you can't all join in now. You can play only after he catches me, *okayyy*?' he told them.

'What rubbish!' said Kaliya's wife. 'Surround the boy!' she told the other snakes.

Just as they were about to catch him, Krishna leapt over the snakes and moved so quickly that they ended up bumping against one another. They lay wriggling on the riverbed in a confused heap, disoriented from the impact. Kaliya, too, was dizzy from trying to follow Krishna's swift movements.

'Boy, where are you?' the giant snake said angrily. But before he knew it, Krishna had hopped on top of one of his hoods.

'Hey! Get down!' Kaliya said, enraged. He moved violently to shake Krishna off, but the little boy had balanced himself brilliantly. As Kaliya took a second to catch his breath, the little boy brought out his flute, tucked in his cummerbund, and began playing a melodious tune.

'Stop that noise! Get down!' Kaliya once again tried to shake him off, but the boy started dancing on his hood instead! Continuing to play the flute, he leapt from one head to another in perfect rhythm.

He was a child, but every little movement of his petite feet felt like a blow to Kaliya's massive head. 'How dare you hit Kal...*cough, cough!*' Each time Krishna jumped on one of his heads, Kaliya was forced to spit out his own venom. By the time the snake coughed out all his venom, the water had turned several shades darker.

All that dancing soon caused Kaliya's hoods to bleed. On the riverbank above, Yashoda, Krishna's friends, the milkmaids and the villagers saw a red stream gushing out, mixing with the black waters of the river. Their hearts sank as they expected the worst.

On the riverbed, Kaliya's family, who had regained their senses by then, rushed to the spot where Krishna continued to dance on Kaliya's heads. 'Please spare Kaliya!' the snake's wife cried. 'We will leave Vrindavan forever!'

Krishna stopped dancing. 'Oh! Then I will go play with my friends now. But we like our river clean. It's *sooo* dirty, look!' He frowned, pointing to the dark waters around.

'Kaliya will clean it for you, boy,' the snake said, looking exhausted and relieved.

'*Okayyy*, I want to go home,' Krishna said.

Kaliya rose above the waters slowly. Krishna was still dancing over the snake's head, but this time, the boy's steps were so light that Kaliya could hardly feel them.

When the mighty snake emerged out of the water, the people on the banks were stunned. Krishna was swaying on Kaliya's head, holding his thick tail in one hand. Yashoda cried inconsolably after seeing that her son was safe.

As Krishna stepped onto the banks, Kaliya bowed his heads to the boy and said, 'Kaliya is sorry for spoiling your river. Kaliya will go away.'

'Bye!' Krishna said and ran into his mother's arms.

By the next morning, the family of snakes had cleaned the entire river, and no trace of venom remained in it. Vrindavan's inhabitants returned to its banks.

Soon, a familiar musical voice rang out. 'Let's play hide-and-seek today, *okayyy*?'

Connecting the Dots...

Krishna, an avatar of Vishnu, is believed to have been born in Mathura in Braj. Just a few kilometres away lies Vrindavan, the place where he spent much of his childhood. A town in Braj, it is located in present-day Uttar Pradesh. The entire region is dotted with temples dedicated to the god. The waterbody that Krishna had succeeded in cleansing by defeating Kaliya is the River Yamuna, which flows through the region even today.

The Celestial River

Legend has it that the *saptarishi* (as the seven sages Atri, Bharadwaja, Gautama, Jamdagni, Kashyapa, Vashishtha and Vishwamitra were known) prayed to Goddess Yamuna to live among them on Prithvi Lok.

Happy with their penance, Yamuna flowed as a stream from Deva Lok to Mount Kalinda. However, when people couldn't settle along her banks, because it was freezing cold on the mountain, she requested her father, Surya (the sun god), to help her.

Surya shot a fiery ray towards a rock at the bottom of Mount Kalinda. So, when Yamuna flowed down to this spot from the cold mountain, her waters magically turned hot. And that is how people could bathe in and use her sacred waters.

Goddess Yamuna is depicted as holding a water pot and riding on the back of a turtle.

The Curious Course of the Yamuna

The Yamuna originates at Saptarishi Kund, a glacial lake formed by the melting snow of the glaciers in Uttarakhand's Garhwal Himalayan range. The lake's waters flow off Mount Kalinda as cool waterfalls and emerge at Surya Kund, near the Yamunotri Temple, several thousand feet below, as a hot water spring.

It is believed that this is where the Indian plate collided with the Eurasian plate millions of years ago. This caused the water flowing over this land to come in contact with the hot core of the earth below, only to rise up again as a hot water spring. These waters then flow from Uttarakhand into Himachal Pradesh, Haryana, Delhi and Uttar Pradesh as the cool Yamuna River.

Also known as Jumna or Jamna, Yami and Kalindi, the river follows a course that is around 1,376 kilometres long. In fact, the Yamuna is among the largest tributaries of the Ganges. The two rivers meet at Allahabad, a sacred city in Uttar Pradesh which is now known as Prayagraj.

Interestingly, Goddess Yamuna's connection with the turtle is not just limited to mythology. The Yamuna River basin is indeed an important habitat for many turtle species. Trafficking of turtles has put their populations at risk. They are poached not just for their meat, but also because of the belief that different parts of the turtle can cure various ailments.

Apart from this, their survival, just like that of the Taj Mahal, mainly depends on the river's condition.

The Dying Symbol of an Immortal Romance

The Yamuna inspired the Mughal emperor Shah Jahan to build the Taj Mahal on its banks in Agra, to show his love for his deceased wife, Mumtaz Mahal. The monument was built such that its form was reflected, in all its pristine glory, in the waters of the river, which flowed past it. And when he was held captive by his son Aurangzeb, Shah Jahan spent his final days watching the reflection of the gorgeous Taj in a specially made mirror that adorned a wall in his prison chamber.

However, the Yamuna now reflects more than just the Taj Mahal; it also mirrors the dark shadow that industrialization has cast on it. No gigantic snake lives there today and yet, the river is black from the millions of litres of human waste and industrial effluents released into it from surrounding areas. It has become impossible for marine life to thrive in its toxic waters. The Yamuna is in such an alarming condition that some environmentalists even call it a 'dead river'.

The Yamuna flows as a testament to Shah Jahan's love for Mumtaz Mahal, but did you know that an entire island celebrates the romantic tale of Krishna and Rukmini?

9

The Land between Two Rivers

Majuli

Dear Krishna,

My brother, Rukmi, wants me to marry his friend, Prince Shishupala. I implore you to come to our kingdom and take me away. But there's no need for a battle. We will be visiting the Girija Temple on the coming full moon day, an hour before noon. If your love for me is as true as mine is for you, meet me there. I will be waiting.

Yours forever,

Princess Rukmini

As a child, Krishna had not only defeated Kaliya, but many other demons as well – from a ferocious monster and a human-eating crane to one disguised as a calf. The young boy had also defeated his cruel uncle Kamsa, the king of Mathura.

Krishna grew up to be a wise young man. The stories of his valour and heroic deeds reached far and wide, impressing many, including Princess Rukmini. She was the daughter of Bhishmaka, the king of Bhishmaknagar.

Bhishmaknagar was in a region that saw the land's sunrise first every morning, while Dwarka (Krishna's kingdom) was in a region where the sun set last every evening. Even though they lived miles apart, Rukmini and Krishna fell in love, through the stories they had heard about each other. Bhishmaka was happy with the match, but Rukmini's brother, Rukmi, did not approve of Krishna. So, he went ahead and arranged the marriage of his sister with his friend, Prince Shishupala of the Chedi kingdom.

An angry and anxious Rukmini sent a messenger to Dwarka. After hearing the message, Krishna smiled and turned to his elder brother, Balarama. 'Okay, get ready, we have a long journey ahead of us.'

On the appointed day, Rukmini waited nervously, but there was no sign of Krishna. She wondered if the messenger had reached him in time. Just as she approached the steps of the Girija Temple, she saw a chariot in the distance.

Tearing through the dust, a form appeared, just as she had imagined. 'Krishna, I knew you'd come!' she cried out.

Balarama, who was Krishna's charioteer for this journey, made sure not to stop the vehicle even when they neared the temple's steps. He swerved expertly while Krishna helped Rukmini climb into the moving vehicle.

Unfortunately, Shishupala spotted them. 'Follow them!' he yelled at his charioteer. Rukmi, who had also reached the temple by then, joined the chase. 'How dare you abduct my sister, Krishna?' he snarled, catching up to their chariot.

'I know you don't want us to fight your brother, but…' Krishna told Rukmini.

'…we have no other choice,' Balarama completed, seeing Krishna hesitate.

Needless to say, Krishna won the ensuing battle and took his bride away. After travelling for a while, they halted at a place called Malinithan, where Shiva and Parvati had been waiting for them.

'What took you so long?' Parvati asked.

'Rukmini refused to come with me until I'd defeated her brother!' Krishna joked.

'Here are your garlands… Parvati made them herself,' Shiva said, handing them over to the couple.

'They're so colourful, and so fragrant,' Rukmini said, admiring the intricately woven, sweet-smelling flowers.

'I'm impressed too! You should be called "Malini",' Krishna said to Parvati, for the name meant 'mistress of gardens'.

'Such a lovely name! Thank you, Krishna,' Parvati replied.

Krishna and Rukmini exchanged the garlands and made a single vow to each other: 'I'm yours forever!'

Rukmini didn't have to worry about being forced into a marriage with Shishupala anymore, but she didn't want another unnecessary battle. So, after spending some time at Shiva and Parvati's garden home, the newly-wed couple decided to travel to Dwarka as quickly as possible.

'The journey will be long, Rukmini. Let's stop over at the next place that catches your eye,' Krishna told his wife, but she was already fast asleep.

On reaching a tranquil island that was in the middle of a wide river basin, Krishna woke her up gently. He thought it would be a good place to stop at and rest for a while. When the princess woke up, she was struck by the beauty of the island. 'Oh! Have we reached Dwarka already?' she asked Krishna.

Krishna laughed and replied, 'No, we haven't.'

Looking around, he realized that this land, which was truly as picturesque as his kingdom, had been formed by the merging and splitting of two rivers. 'But you know what, Rukmini? Just as these two rivers have created and embraced this island, the people of this region will celebrate us and preserve the story of our love forever. And one day, this exquisite land will come to be known as the second Dwarka,' he said.

As they watched the sunset together, the couple knew that they had found a new home, away from both their kingdoms.

Connecting the Dots...

Bhishmaknagar, Bhishmaka's kingdom, is said to have been located where present-day Arunachal Pradesh stands. Shishupala's Chedi kingdom is believed to have been close to present-day Bundelkhand in Madhya Pradesh. Krishna and Rukmini got married in Malinithan, which is also in Arunachal Pradesh. The couple halted in the Brahmaputra River basin, on a riverine island called Majuli. Situated in Assam today, Majuli Island is indeed known as the second Dwarka.

The Dance of Rukmini

The Idu-Mishmi people of Arunachal Pradesh believe that Rukmini belonged to their tribe. Not all tribespeople and experts agree with this view, however. Some feel that the tale from Hindu mythology has been merged with the cultural beliefs of the Idu-Mishmi community to create this impression. But even today, some Idu-Mishmi groups enact the episode of *Rukmini haran* ('the abduction of Rukmini') through their folk theatre and dance traditions.

An Unusual Land

In Assamese, the word *majuli* refers to 'the land between two parallel rivers'. The Brahmaputra flows to the north of this island, while the Dihing runs along to its south. And that's what gives it the name Majuli. It is no ordinary place – Majuli has been featured in the *Guinness Book of World Records* as the largest river island in the world!

Several years ago, a major flood caused by an earthquake forced the Brahmaputra and its tributaries to change their course. Until then, the Brahmaputra and the Dihing used to run parallel to each other. But when the Brahmaputra's course changed, it began flowing diagonally in the Dihing's path. This change made the Dihing flow into the Brahmaputra, thus becoming one of its largest tributaries. Further, the two merged rivers moved apart some distance away, and then merged again at a point called Dihingmukh.

The sand deposited by the two rivers and their tributaries, where the waters separated before meeting again, transformed into a water-locked tract of land. This is what we know as the riverine island of Majuli. The silt deposits also created islets or small islands called *chaporis* all around the main island. Far from being an empty, unoccupied landmass today, Majuli is home to more than 200 populated villages!

But the frequent flooding of the Brahmaputra, even on the not-so-rainy days, is eating up Majuli, bit by bit. In the past century, the island has shrunk by hundreds of square kilometres, as the water regularly erodes the soil.

The shrinking of the island also poses a threat to a distinct culture that has taken root in Majuli – one that celebrates Rukmini and Krishna, just as the king of Dwarka had foretold!

For the Love of Vishnu

The idea of worshipping Vishnu and his avatars is called Vaishnavism. In the fifteenth century, a spiritual leader named Sankardeva, along with his disciple Madhabdeva, brought the concept of neo-Vaishnavism to Majuli. He observed that people from scheduled castes, tribal communities and economically backward sections were often not allowed into certain places of worship. Through neo-Vaishnavism, Sankardeva taught that all people had an equal right to worship the god. To help people understand these teachings, he set up a large network of *sattras* (monasteries) across the villages of Majuli that inculcated devotion for Vishnu and Krishna among the people of the region, particularly through arts, music and dance. One such devotional art form is the Sattriya dance, which presents episodes related to the two gods, especially the love story of Rukmini and Krishna.

With the people of Majuli showing Krishna the same kind of affection that the Yadava people of Dwarka showered upon him, Majuli eventually came to be known as the second Dwarka.

Flowing waters changed their paths to create the second Dwarka, but did you know that the waters of a sea eventually swallowed the original Dwarka?

10

The Keeper of a Lost Kingdom

Sindhu Sagar

The divine architect, Vishwakarma, had built a dazzling city for Krishna, Balarama and the Yadava people on the shores of a vast sea called Sindhu Sagar. Named Dwarka, meaning 'gateway', the kingdom literally looked like the entrance to paradise, with its mesmerizing gardens, lavish palaces and homes made of gold, and enchanting views of the moonrise and sunset.

Krishna brought his wife Rukmini to this divine city after their wedding, and they started their life together.

One day, Shiva and Brahma appeared before him.

'Have you forgotten that you are Vishnu too?' Brahma asked Krishna.

'But you two are managing the universe so well. Do you really need me?' Krishna said, smiling.

'Of course we do!' Shiva said.

'We're incomplete without you, you know that. That's why we've come to take you back with us,' Brahma said.

Krishna sighed. 'All right, give me seven days. I have some unfinished business to attend to.'

In one of his avatars, Vishnu appeared on Prithvi Lok as Krishna, the son of Devaki and Vasudev. Devaki was the sister of the cruel ruler of Mathura, Kamsa, who had overthrown his own father, Ugrasen, and crowned himself king.

When Kamsa's behaviour towards the people of his kingdom worsened, a voice from heaven announced, 'Don't think you are invincible, foolish Kamsa! The eighth son of Devaki will defeat you and end your horrible rule over Mathura.'

Kamsa promptly imprisoned Devaki and Vasudev. Not wanting to take any chances, he killed their first six sons as soon as they were born. Through a strange miracle, the couple's seventh son, Balarama, was born to another woman called Rohini, even though, *technically*, Devaki was the boy's mother. (Yes, it's confusing, but that's a story for another time!) Balarama was born in the home of Vasudev's friend Nanda, the chief of the Yadavas, who lived in the village of Gokul in Mathura. As the boy was born in their home, Nanda and his wife, Yashoda, raised Balarama as their own son.

When Kamsa realized that the seventh child had vanished from Devaki's womb, he stationed more guards outside the prison cell and told them, 'If something strange happens, call me immediately!'

The night when Devaki gave birth to her eighth son, Krishna, the gods from Deva Lok came to her rescue. All the prison guards fell asleep and the prison gates opened magically, allowing Vasudev to escape with the baby. Vasudev headed straight to Nanda's home in Gokul. Leaving Krishna safely with him, Vasudev brought back the baby girl who had been born to Nanda and Yashoda that very night. As soon as Vasudev entered the prison cell, the gates shut automatically and the guards woke up.

One of them immediately informed Kamsa that the eighth child had been born. When Kamsa stormed into the prison cell, he was taken aback. 'What's this? It should have been a boy!' he thundered.

'*B-but*, a girl has been born. You are in no danger from her!' Devaki cried, fearing for the baby's safety.

'Aha! The gods are playing with me, but I won't fall for this. Boy or girl, this is the eighth child. And if she will grow up to be a threat to my life, she needn't live that long at all!'

Saying this, Kamsa flung the baby against a wall. Vasudev and Devaki screamed in horror. But to everyone's surprise, the baby girl didn't hit the wall. Instead, she transformed into a goddess. Seated on a roaring lion and holding a sword in one of her four hands, Goddess Katyayani (a form of Goddess Durga) hovered over them.

'O foolish Kamsa, Vishnu has already taken birth as your nephew Krishna, and he is safe,' she said, laughing loudly. '*He* is the eighth son of Devaki. Balarama, the seventh son of Devaki, is safe too. Don't ever imagine that you can escape your end.'

The goddess vanished, but her shrill laughter continued to ring in Kamsa's ears. He didn't show it, but he was clearly shaken.

'Pah! Nonsensical drama!' he muttered and left.

Meanwhile, Krishna grew up as the son of Nanda and Yashoda in Gokul. Soon, the day arrived when he and Kamsa had a face-off. Krishna was still a boy, but he was much stronger than Kamsa. The fight ended with the nephew defeating his evil uncle just as the divine voice had prophesied.

Krishna released his parents and his grandfather, Ugrasen, from prison. He then made Ugrasen the king of Mathura once again and had Vishwakarma build a new city for him and the Yadava people. And that is how Krishna came to live in Dwarka.

All was going well until Brahma and Shiva paid him a visit. After the two gods left, Krishna slipped into a melancholic mood. He stared at the silhouettes of the gardens and houses of the city, formed against the bright moonlight. In the distance, the reflection of the full moon was clearly visible in the dark waters of the Sindhu Sagar. Krishna took out his flute and played a soul-stirring tune.

'I need your help, Sindhu,' Krishna whispered to the quiet sea.

As if on cue, the weather changed in Dwarka from the next day onwards. Animals and birds moved about uneasily.

Krishna addressed the people of the city. 'This is going to be hard, but all of you must leave Dwarka,' he urged.

The shocked crowds began to murmur among themselves.

'Quiet,' Balarama said. 'Krishna would never say anything without a reason. Listen.'

'Dwarka is not safe anymore. Go to a place that is high enough and away from the sea,' Krishna instructed.

'But what about you, Krishna? You're coming with us, aren't you?' an old woman asked, feeling a sense of foreboding. 'You aren't going away, Krishna, are you?'

Krishna swallowed the lump in his throat. 'I'll always be with all of you,' he said quietly.

Tearfully, the people of Dwarka moved to higher ground. But in the next few days, they became wayward without their leader. They fought bitterly amongst themselves, and destroyed each other's lives.

'This is not the city I created,' Krishna told Balarama sadly, staring at Dwarka's empty streets. A week had passed since Brahma and Shiva's visit.

'It's time, Krishna,' Balarama replied, patting his back.

Krishna walked slowly towards the seashore, followed by Balarama. Dark clouds filled the sky, like a gloomy veil covering Dwarka. Stepping into the waters of the Sindhu Sagar, Krishna said, 'Keep Dwarka safe, okay?' and vanished into thin air.

The sea slowly crept into Dwarka. Flowing in further and further, its waters rose and swallowed Dwarka whole, like a giant fish.

When the remaining Yadava people, who had taken refuge on higher ground, looked in the direction of their golden city, all they could see were the bobbing waters of the Sindhu Sagar.

Connecting the Dots...

Sindhu Sagar was one of the older names of the Arabian Sea. Krishna's Dwarka was built by Vishwakarma facing this sea, on one edge of what we know today as the Gulf of Kutch near Gujarat.

A Divine Brotherhood

It is believed that Sheshnag, the thousand-headed snake on whose coiled body and tail Vishnu rests, was born as Krishna's elder brother, Balarama. Along with Krishna, he too left for Vaikunth, Vishnu's divine abode, from the shores of the Sindhu Sagar.

An Ancient Trade Route

The Sindhu Sagar was probably among the first set of trade routes discovered by humans. Traders and seafarers from early civilizations across the world travelled to faraway lands by boats and ships. It was through the Sindhu Sagar that traders from Mesopotamia (an early civilization that was located where present-day Iraq stands) and ancient Egypt carried on trade with the people of the Indus Valley Civilization, which flourished in the north-western regions of present-day India and Pakistan. This civilization gets its name from the River Indus, which flowed through it. In Sanskrit, the Indus was called the Sindhu – it is said that the sea was also named so because the Indus or Sindhu has been one of the major rivers that emptied its waters into it.

Many centuries later, this sea route became the stronghold of Arab merchants. And so, the waters took on their name and became the Arabian Sea.

Over the years, the sea level of not just the Arabian Sea but of all waterbodies on earth has constantly been changing. Human activities such as deforestation, construction and mining, which have led to the melting of glaciers and the depletion of groundwater, are the major causes for sea level change.

It is said that the surging water levels of the Sindhu Sagar led to the sinking of Dwarka. The sea, however, seems to have kept its promise to Krishna, for Dwarka never really disappeared. It has always remained safely hidden in the deep waters of the Arabian Sea.

The Discovery of Dwarka

Since the 1930s, researchers had been trying to find clues to Krishna's lost kingdom. After three decades, when marine archaeologists carried out excavations, they found Dwarka intact, submerged a short distance from Gujarat's coastline, in the Arabian Sea. Streets, walls and boulders were found during subsequent excavations conducted between 1983 and 1990. The discovery of stone anchors showed that Dwarka had trade ships coming in and leaving from its shores.

Over the years, several civilizations in the region have built and rebuilt the city of Dwarka – at least six times at last count. The Dwarka that exists in Gujarat today is different and newer than the one found underwater. Experts say that the city may have had to be reconstructed or shifted over time due to the changing sea levels caused by tectonic plate movements and evolving climatic conditions.

Dating (the process of assigning an age or time period to something) the discovered sunken city has been a complex process. Researchers are still trying to find out if the underwater city is, indeed, Krishna's Dwarka, or if it was a city built much later, perhaps when the Arabs began trading with the Indian subcontinent.

The Sindhu Sagar drowned Dwarka to preserve it on Krishna's orders, but did you know that there was another sea that took it upon itself to protect a kingdom?

11

Born with a Splash

Chilika

'How dare you?' Raktabahu gritted his teeth, glaring at the sea, his eyes red with rage.

As if afraid, the sea retreated.

'Hah, you can't escape me!' Raktabahu said, slashing through the waters with his sword.

The waters receded a little more.

'How far can you go? I really want to see!' he said, thrilled that the mighty sea was so afraid of him. He kept walking ahead.

The sea now parted, revealing a dry path. Raktabahu laughed and called out to his army, 'Come on! The foolish sea is so scared...let's see where it's planning to escape to.'

'I don't think that's a good idea,' the commander of his army said cautiously.

'Fool! Just do as I say!' Raktabahu roared.

With the army marching in, the sea cowered further.

A prosperous kingdom thrived on the shores of an expansive sea. A well-known temple dedicated to the deity Jagannath (an avatar of Vishnu) and his siblings, Balabhadra and Subhadra, stood on the shores. The sea was used to quietly watching the devotees, who came from far-off places to pray at the shore temple. Never had it imagined that a pirate king would enter the kingdom someday to try and loot the temple and steal its deities. But Raktabahu, with his large pirate army, had set sail with this very intention.

'Drop anchor here!' Raktabahu ordered his crew when his ships were a few nautical miles away from the temple.

'We are still far away from the shore,' his commander replied.

'Don't be a fool! If they see our ships on the horizon now, they'll have time to prepare and save the temple's treasures,' he yelled at the commander. 'We'll wait here and move in tomorrow, past midnight – just before the new moon appears. The sea is our cover!'

But the sea could not let the people of the land down. It had to do something to protect the deities!

Early next morning, when the temple's chief priest visited the shore, he was taken aback. 'What's all this garbage? Who has been polluting the sea? This is so wrong,' he said to himself, looking at the litter that had washed onto the shore.

'People no longer respect nature…' he muttered, and then stopped. 'O Lord Jagannath! Tell me it's not true!'

He ran back to the temple and rounded up the other priests. 'Quick, we must go to the palace! We are going to be attacked!'

'How do you know that?' one of the priests asked.

'The sea! It has sent us a message by washing ashore litter. Everyone in our kingdom respects the sea. Nobody…not even the devotees who come from other regions have ever polluted its waters. This means that there are ships lurking in the sea, but we can't see them yet! And from the amount of garbage that I saw on the shore, I think there are several ships,' the chief priest explained.

The group rushed to the palace to inform the king. 'Pirates! Pirates are hiding somewhere in the sea, and I think they are coming for the temple's treasures, Your Majesty,' the chief priest announced, panting.

The king was worried, but he showed no panic. 'Inform the town's people, ask them to evacuate,' he told the royal messenger.

He then turned to the priests and said, 'We must move the deities.'

The priests looked at each other. 'How can the gods be moved from their temple…their home? O Lord Jagannath! What kind of solution is this?' the chief priest mumbled under his breath.

'We should not underestimate the enemy,' the king said, guessing what the priest was thinking. 'We can surely fight the pirates, but our first responsibility is to keep the deities and our people safe.'

Seeing that there was no other way, the priests agreed. The soldiers reached the temple in no time. They placed the three idols on a large temple cart and moved them to another location.

Later that night, Raktabahu's ships glided stealthily towards the shore. Before the sun's rays broke through the bleak sky, the pirate king stood on the beach, right in front of the temple.

The commander looked around and said, 'It's eerily quiet here, even for this hour of the morning.'

'Hah, fool! They must all be asleep!' Raktabahu snorted. 'When they wake up, they'll see that their gods and the temple treasures are gone.' He rubbed his hands excitedly.

'Umm, I don't think so…' the commander said slowly. 'I think they have all escaped!'

'Fool, fool, fool! How could they have escaped?' Raktabahu glared at him. But as he sprinted up and down the shore, he realized that his commander was right. There was no one around. 'How? How–how–how?'

'Surely, the temple's priests would never leave their gods alone and run away,' he said, marching towards the temple.

However, not a soul was in sight within the precincts either. With great difficulty, his army broke down the door to the inner sanctum of the temple, only to find it completely empty!

'What? The gods are gone? *How did they know?*' Raktabahu fumed. Then, turning to his commander, he said, '*Someone* has betrayed *me*!'

'No, no, no! It wasn't me, or any of our men,' the commander said.

'Then who?' Raktabahu exclaimed, punching his own hand.

The first rays of the sun fell upon some objects on the shore.

'What's that?' Raktabahu asked, going closer to inspect them. Seeing that it was nothing but litter, he was just about to turn away when the realization dawned on him. 'No wonder! This litter is from *our* ships. Aren't these leaf-plates the ones our men had their meals in?' he yelled.

'*Y-yes*,' the commander replied hesitantly. 'The waters have washed them ashore.'

Turning angrily towards the sea, Raktabahu shouted, '*You! You* have betrayed me!'

Slashing the waves with his sword, he moved towards the sea, which kept retreating, letting Raktabahu and his army further in. The pirate king laughed. 'Coward!'

In that moment, without any warning, the waters, now towering over them, erupted.

Raktabahu gasped. Before they could all run back to the shore, the wall of water came crashing down, swallowing the ships, the army and a distraught Raktabahu whole. It descended and flowed back towards the shore with such force that some of the water spilled over onto the nearby land, forming a lake.

It was over in a matter of minutes, and calm returned to the shore again in the form of gentle waves. The sea had succeeded in protecting its land, people and the temple's deities.

Connecting the Dots...

The sea that fought Raktabahu's army all by itself was the Bay of Bengal. The inland pool, which was created by the surging waters of the bay, is located in Odisha and is known today as the Chilika Lake.

Being closely connected to the Bay of Bengal, the Chilika Lake was a harbour in ancient times. Puri, one of the districts of Odisha bordering the lake, became a prosperous port thanks to its maritime trade. But when silt deposits began settling at the mouth of the lake, it became difficult for large ships to enter and anchor at the lake port. Eventually, the region's sea trade suffered and slowly vanished.

The shrine that Raktabahu wanted to loot is the famous Shri Jagannath Temple located in Puri. While Raktabahu was the first to try and raid this shore temple, historians have documented that the shrine and the city have faced the threat of invasion and plunder 18 times!

The Greater Force

In the late 1700s, Harisevak Mansingh, the king of Bankad (now Banpur town in Odisha), was attacked by the king of Khurda (now Odisha's Khordha district). After being defeated, when Harisevak shifted to Parikud, an island in the Chilika Lake, the Khurda king came there with his army to attack Bhagirathi Mansingh, Harisevak's son.

As his army approached the island, the Khurda king spotted some silhouettes on the Chilika Lake from a distance. 'Looks like a large battalion is marching towards us from Parikud. Our army is too small to win against them,' the king said to his commander.

Changing his mind, the Khurda king instructed his men to retreat.

Little did he know that the army of silhouettes protecting the region was *not* made up of soldiers. It was a group of large birds that had migrated to the lake in the winter! Nature had once again outwitted an invader! These birds are believed to have been greater flamingos, which still visit the Chilika Lake in the hundreds.

The Blue Lagoon

Surrounded by the Ganjam, Khordha and Puri districts of Odisha on one side and the Bay of Bengal on the other, the Chilika Lake is Asia's largest brackish water lake. While waters from 52 rivulets and streams fill this unique coastal lagoon with freshwater, the brackish (or salty) water comes into it from the bay. A coastal lagoon is a waterbody with slightly salty water that is separated from the sea by a sandbank.

In the Pleistocene Era – around 2.6 million years to 11,700 years ago – the whole lake and the land surrounding it were part of the Bay of Bengal. Around 6,000–7,000 years ago, the sea levels changed, causing the bay's waters to recede and reveal a new coastline. Over the years, water currents, the action of wind on the sand, and changing land and water positions formed a sandbank some distance away from the new coastline, thus separating a pool of water from the sea. This newly formed pool became the Chilika.

Initially, the sandbank (a raised stretch of land created underwater by sand deposits) had an opening that was about a kilometre long. Through this opening, the salty water from the bay mixed with the lake's freshwater. But a few thousand years ago, newer sand deposits closed the gap, separating the lake from the sea completely.

The Custodians of the Lake

In 1991, a special government agency called the Chilika Development Authority was set up to preserve the lake's ecosystem. But in 1993, due to excessive siltation, the lake was listed as 'threatened' in the Montreux Record, an international data system that keeps track of lakes and wetlands undergoing major changes.

In 2000, the lake mouth (which had closed completely by then) was opened up by the Chilika Development Authority using a process called 'desilting' or 'desiltation' – in this, machines are used to artificially remove the collected silt from a waterbody. This was done as the inflow of seawater into Chilika is important to preserve the lake and the aquatic life that thrives in and around it.

In 2002, the Chilika Lake became the first conserved site from Asia to have its name crossed out of the list of threatened lakes in the Montreux Record! Now, that's quite an achievement, isn't it?

The Bay of Bengal and the Chilika Lake have been natural guardians. But did you know that there was a sea which incurred the wrath of Vishnu for being destructive?

12

The Mighty Guardians

Himalayas

'What is wrong with this sea?' Vishnu shouted angrily.

As if in response to Vishnu, the waves flowed far into the shore. Then, sweeping away a crab that was busy digging a hole in the sand, it receded.

Having noticed what the sea had done, Vishnu said to it, 'You seem to love playing the "swallowing game", huh? Watch this now!'

He closed his eyes, opened his mouth wide and inhaled.

Vishnu had grown rather fond of the Prithvi Lok that Brahma had created. He built himself a cosy home close to a vast blue sea once and decided to stay there for a while.

One day, a pair of seagulls arrived at the seashore. The female seagull chose a safe spot away from the sea to make a nest – it was time for her to lay her eggs. But just as she finished laying them, the seawater sped ashore and consumed the seagull's eggs in a single gulp. The shocked seagulls fluttered around for a while, circling the place where the eggs had been just a few moments ago. They screeched and screeched, but the eggs were gone. After mourning for a while, the couple flew away.

A year later, the two seagulls returned to the same shore. Fearing that the sea would swallow her eggs again, the mother gull chose a spot further away, near some rocks. The eggs were laid. Once again, before the seagulls could rejoice, the sea groaned, lunged forward and gobbled up the eggs in a single swallow. The dejected seagulls fluttered and cried out, and then quietly flew away.

The next year, the seagulls came to the seashore again. This time, the female seagull laid her eggs far, far away from the sea, high up in the rocks, hoping that the waters wouldn't steal her little ones. But the waves twirled and danced, and in a giant leap, took away the eggs all at once.

Heartbroken and unable to bear the grief of seeing their unborn young ones being washed away year after year, the seagulls flew straight to Vishnu's seaside home. He was still living there, as luck would have it. The birds told him all that had happened.

The annoyed god reached the seashore, and when he saw the sea wash away a poor crab, he couldn't take it anymore. He opened his mouth and began to inhale slowly.

The sea realized what Vishnu was up to. At first, it tried to resist, but it knew that it was no match for the god's powers. So it apologized to the seagulls and pleaded with Vishnu for forgiveness, even as its waters were drawn towards the god's open mouth.

But Vishnu heard nothing except the sound of his own breath, much like the sound trapped in a conch shell on the shore.

In no time, he had gulped down all the water in the sea. In its place, as far as the seagulls could see, only land was visible now.

'Happy?' Vishnu asked the birds, who went around him many times, squawking, to thank him. They were thrilled that the god had taught the arrogant sea a lesson – its waters would not destroy any more lives.

Meanwhile, Vishnu was exhausted. 'Drinking up the sea has drained me out,' he said to himself.

Too tired to go home, he stretched himself out on the soft shore and fell asleep. It was a slumber so deep that he missed an entire one-sided battle that took place around him – the match between the freshly emerged land and his old enemy, the asura Hiranyaksha!

Hiranyaksha, who had been passing by, had witnessed all that had transpired between the sea, the gulls and Vishnu. He had been waiting for a moment like this – to show Vishnu how powerful he was.

'Creating new lands, eh, Vishnu?' he said to the sleeping god. 'Come on, get up and fight me! You know I won't attack a sleeping enemy!'

His eyes gleamed when Vishnu didn't budge. He knew the god had no energy left in him.

'*Tsk tsk tsk*... How can you sleep when I, the great Hiranyaksha, am here to destroy the very earth that you have just created?' And he thrust a strong fist into the ground. But Vishnu didn't stir.

Hiranyaksha went on and on. He tore the heart of the earth out. He broke it bit by bit. He threw rocks here and upturned tonnes of mud there.

When he was done, it seemed as though the land's many limbs were strewn all over and arranged into tall heaps. The whole place was a complete mess.

The asura dusted off his silk robes and his hands, went close to the still sleeping Vishnu and whispered in his ears, 'Sweet dreams, Vishnu. You're going to wake up to a bitter nightmare!'

Laughing wildly, Hiranyaksha walked away.

In his sleep, Vishnu smiled.

The broken pieces of the earth, which looked like nothing more than giant heaps of rubble, suddenly merged together. They transformed into a chain of majestic mountains with peaks that rose so high that they almost touched the sky.

The region that was home to a sea until that morning had now become a mountain range.

Connecting the Dots...

The sea that Vishnu swallowed is believed to have been the ancient Tethys Sea, and the mountain range that formed in its place, the Himalayas! In Sanskrit, Himalaya means the 'abode of snow', a name it gets because of its snow-capped peaks and glaciers. A part of the Himalayan Mountain Range, the Hindu Kush–Himalayan belt, which spans many countries, is also called the Third Pole (the other two being the North Pole and the South Pole), due to the large volumes of snow found here.

Standing Tall

Mountain ranges often protect countries from possible enemy attacks. The Himalayas too guard the six countries they run through – Afghanistan, Bhutan, China, India, Nepal and Pakistan. It is extremely difficult to trek up some of the Himalayan crests, for they are among the highest in the world.

From a Vast Sea to a Snowy Abode

As you may know by now, the vast Tethys Sea was located in the region where the Himalayas are today. The impact of the Indian plate colliding with the Eurasian plate caused subduction, a process in which one plate goes below another plate.

When this happens, the plates tend to bend or fold, leading to a pile-up of rocks and sediments, much like the ones created by Hiranyaksha in the tale! Such an accumulated mass is called an accretionary wedge. The sediments continue to pile up as tall heaps, eventually forming mountains or entire mountain ranges with high peaks. The Himalayas too were formed in this way, with the subduction of the Indian plate below the Eurasian plate. The Tethys Sea slowly began shrinking due to subduction, its seabed rose, and eventually, its waters vanished.

As several of the Himalayan peaks soar to high altitudes, the temperature in these regions is extremely cold, especially during the winter. At such times, the water vapour in the atmosphere turns into ice crystals – when many such tiny crystals stick together, a snowflake is formed. Billions of snowflakes then cause snowfall, and create snowcaps over these mountain peaks. When the climate becomes warmer, the same snow begins to melt and flow downwards in the form of water streams, giving life to many rivers in the country.

The King of the Mountains

Legend has it that Himavan, the father of the goddess Parvati, was the king of the Himalayas. What makes the mountains so sacred is that they guard many secrets and regional legends, such as the tale of the Mani Mahesh Peak and the lake. But some say that it is another king who rules these mountains today – the gigantic yeti!

For many years, people from around the world have believed that a strange creature, which looks like a large apeman with whitish-grey fur, has been living hidden in the Himalayan mountains. Several explorers have claimed to have seen an elusive figure similar to the yeti, or found its huge footprints in the snow.

It is hard to say whether this animal truly exists or if it is a myth of the mountains. Until concrete proof is found, the mystery of the yeti will continue to live on among the steep passages of the Himalayas.

The Fossil Wallah and the Beast Legion

The yeti is not the only fascinating beast to have roamed these mountains. In the 1830s, a British engineer named Captain Proby Thomas Cautley came to India to work on the construction of the Ganges Canal and the repairing of the eastern Yamuna Canal. During the course of his work, he stumbled onto something invaluable on the slopes of the Shivalik Hills in the lower Himalayan Range in Himachal Pradesh – animal fossils!

Initially, Cautley was upset that he had failed to dig up the fossil of the *Sivatherium giganteum*, a tall and big giraffe-like species with four horns, which lived in this region a long time ago. Later, when he found the bones and jaws of a number of other animals with their joints intact, he decided to dig them up himself. The local people had known about the presence of such bones all along. They had been collecting them for years as they believed that the bones had magical powers.

The region had once been home to the rat, porcupine, hippopotamus, rhinoceros, gharial, crane, tortoise, sabre-toothed tiger and many elephant species (some with tusks that were ten feet long!). These animals were unlike the ones we see around us today – they were, in fact, gigantic beasts! The fossils proved that they had lived along the Shivalik Range around two million to 12 million years ago. While Cautley collected fossils of many of these animals, the remains of the *Sivapithecus*, an ancient ape considered to be the ancestor of human beings, were his most prized discovery.

More than a century after these discoveries were made by Cautley, in 1974, the Geological Survey of India and the Himachal Pradesh government set up Asia's biggest fossil park at the very site where these mysterious creatures had roamed ages ago.

Located in the Sirmaur district's Suketi village, the Siwalik Fossil Park (also called Suketi Fossil Park) has life-size fibreglass models of the giant hippopotamus, mammoth, tortoise and other beasts. While the park's museum has some of the fossils that Cautley unearthed on display, the others were sent to places like the American Museum of Natural History and the British Museum.

In all, Cautley discovered fossils weighing around 40 tonnes, a feat for which he came to be called 'fossil wallah'! And all this has been possible only because the mighty mountain range had preserved these pieces of history in its folds for millions of years.

One with Nature

Many communities see certain geographical features as guardians and protectors, and even have rituals, art forms and festivals revolving around sacred geography.

Others believe that the gods and goddesses (especially the latter) manifest themselves as different natural elements. So if you go by their stories, there's a whole host of goddesses living on earth as rivers, peaks, waterfalls, rocks and caves. These goddesses have the most amazing powers – they can make islands float, devour rocks and trees, and even break the skulls of anyone who dares to offend them!

13

Stories Buried in Snow

Nanda Kot and Roopkund

Remembering her father's words, Princess Nanda kept her sister Sunanda close to her, and ran towards the mountain range that surrounded their kingdom.

'Ah, don't waste my time, princesses! I'll catch up with you sooner or later,' the wicked prince called out.

The sisters hurried up a steep slope, but he was right behind them.

Looking back at him, Nanda did the only thing that she could think of to save herself and Sunanda from becoming the prince's captives.

'My daughter says no, and I stand by her decision. I'm sorry,' the reigning king of the Chand dynasty said to the prince of the Rohilla tribe.

'Sorry?' The prince raised an eyebrow.

The king cleared his throat and repeated, 'My daughter...'

'Oh, I heard you the first time,' the prince drawled. 'How can your daughter say no? Does she know that my army can squash your kingdom in no time? Does she know that you cannot afford to make an enemy of me, if you wish to stay alive?'

Without batting an eyelid, the king repeated, 'My daughter says no, and I stand by her decision. I'm sorry, Prince!'

'Very well, then... Prepare for your worst nightmares to come true!' the prince warned and left.

Nanda was no ordinary princess. She was an incarnation of Goddess Parvati. Having heard about the prince's threat, she walked into her father's chambers, looking furious. 'How *dare* he?'

The king smiled and patted his daughter's head. 'Promise me, Nanda…whatever happens, you will stick to your decision! And make sure that you and Sunanda are always together.'

'Of course I will!' she said.

As the king had expected, the Rohilla prince was back in a few days – this time, with his entire army in tow. The king was ready to fight, even though he knew that this would be a difficult battle to win.

'I will never disrespect the decisions of my daughters,' he said to the commander of his army. 'Nanda is absolutely right. A man who cannot respect a woman's wishes can never make a good companion.'

On the battlefield, Nanda and Sunanda fought alongside their father. Much to the prince's disappointment, the king did not surrender. After a long battle, the prince finally slayed the king and gained control over his kingdom.

Before occupying the throne, however, he wanted to capture the princesses, especially Nanda.

Somehow, the princesses managed to escape to one of the mountains around the kingdom. The Rohilla prince chased them along its steep slope. But then, Nanda did something unexpected in order to keep the promise she had made to her father.

'O mighty mountains,' she called out, 'let us live here forever, as nature…as one of you.'

Both the sisters spread their arms, as if they were hugging the mountain's slope.

The prince was now so close that he had to merely extend his arm to grab hold of Nanda. 'Caught you!' he said, almost touching her shoulder. But to his surprise, Nanda vanished into thin air, and so did Sunanda.

In an instant, the ground began to shake, and the prince lost his balance. As he rolled down the slope, he realized that the mountain had taken the sisters in, for its shape had changed.

Nanda and Sunanda were no longer human beings – they were now mountain peaks!

Connecting the Dots...

People living in the Himalayan regions of Garhwal and Kumaon in Uttarakhand worship the two royal sisters. Since they believe that the duo turned into the twin peaks which loom over the region, those are considered sacred as well. The summits are, naturally, called Sunanda Devi and Nanda Kot ('Nanda's fortress').

The Curse of an Angry Goddess

Once, Shiva and Nanda Devi (as Parvati is called in this region) were travelling through the mountainous terrain, when the goddess suddenly felt thirsty. Shiva thrust his *trishul* into the earth and created a waterbody. As the goddess drank from it, she was happy to see how clearly the waters reflected her beautiful face.

The lake thus came to be called Roopkund (in Hindi, *roop* means 'beauty' and *kund* means 'lake'). However, even though there's beauty in its name, Roopkund has long been associated with the goddess's wrath and the curse of death, as the tale of King Jasdhaval and Queen Balampha tells us.

King Jasdhaval and Queen Balampha were troubled to see their kingdom, Kannauj, face frequent famines. The royal priest prescribed a remedy. 'This seems to be a curse. The only way to save our land is to visit Nanda Kot and seek Nanda Devi's blessings.'

Following his advice, the royal couple undertook a pilgrimage to the peak along with their entourage of soldiers, attendants, and musicians and dancers.

On the way to Nanda Kot, they stopped some distance away from the Roopkund Lake for the night. But instead of following the rules of the pilgrimage, the king called for entertainment.

'Let the music and dancing begin,' he ordered. Through the night, the group enjoyed the performances and disturbed the peace of the place.

Nanda Devi was livid. This was no way to behave during a sacred journey that they had specially undertaken to protect their kingdom. The enraged goddess turned the dancers to stone and sent a terrible hailstorm after the rest of the group.

They ran helter-skelter for a long time, trying to shelter themselves from the heavy hail. But the storm caught up with them at Roopkund Lake. Giant hailstones hit the back of their heads with such force that they just dropped dead – some of them tripped and fell into the lake's icy waters due to the impact, never to be seen again. When the furious winds calmed down, all that remained was a thick blanket of snow covering their lifeless forms.

The Nanda Devi Trail

Nanda Devi's devotees undertake an arduous pilgrimage every 12 years. Carrying a golden idol of Nanda Devi on a palanquin, they walk for more than three weeks, covering around 290 kilometres of the hilly terrain! Known as Nanda Devi Raj Jat Yatra, the journey is a re-enactment of the goddess's wedding parade from her parents' home to Shiva's abode in Mount Kailash.

The route begins at Nauti village in Uttarakhand, and passing through Pathar Nachauni (the place where the punished dancers from Jasdhaval's troupe are believed to still stand as stones), it ends at Roopkund Lake.

Meanwhile, every September, the Nanda Devi Mela is held across Uttarakhand. Processions of the identical-looking goddesses are taken around in a palanquin. The mela or fair is also a celebration of the region's folk arts that are closely connected to the goddesses.

The Twins and the Tempest

The two peaks, which are a part of the Himalayan Range in Uttarakhand, were formed after the Indian plate collided with the Eurasian plate. They are called 'twin peaks' for two reasons. Firstly, they get their names from the sisters Nanda and Sunanda. Secondly, they look like two peaks on either edge of the same mountain, joined by a jagged ridge in between. However, the Nanda Devi Peak or Nanda Kot (situated to the west) is slightly taller than the Sunanda Devi Peak (which is also called Nanda Devi East).

Over the years, the peaks have formed the backdrop for several fatal snowstorms. A snowstorm or blizzard is usually caused by heavy snowfall over a high-altitude region, accompanied by fast, cold winds. Sadly, quite a few people who have been caught in such storms while trekking up the Nanda Kot and Sunanda Devi peaks have lost their lives.

The snowstorms in this region are known to have claimed much more than human lives. In 1965, India carried out a mission to set up a plutonium-powered remote sensing device atop Nanda Kot to watch over neighbouring regions. Plutonium is a radioactive chemical element (a substance that emits energy as electromagnetic waves) and can be extremely dangerous and cause mass destruction. But, due to a blizzard, the team hurriedly returned from Nanda Kot without completing their task.

After they got back, they realized that their equipment, along with the deadly plutonium capsules, had been left behind on the mountain. Months later, when the team returned to the site to look for the equipment, they only found thick sheets of snow instead. The capsules have never been found to this day. It is said that they could still be buried deep within the slopes of the peak. Perhaps the mountain took in the capsules too, just as it had accepted the two sisters as its own! Since the Nanda Kot is one of the glaciers that feeds the Ganga, which flows through Uttarakhand, there is a fear that radiation from the lost capsules may pollute the river. So, its waters are regularly checked for plutonium leakage. However, until any clear signs are found, only Nanda Devi would know where the equipment remains hidden.

Shrouded in Mystery

Like the Mani Mahesh Lake and the Saptarishi Kund, Roopkund is a glacial lake. Located near the Trishul Peak in the Himalayas, it is also called Mystery Lake and Skeleton Lake.

Roopkund is covered in snow for most of the year. When it gets warmer, the snow turns into a clear pool of water, revealing the remnants of ancient skulls and bones on the lakebed and its banks. Radiocarbon dating (a method used to find the age of an object) has established that the bones belong to people from different time periods. When examined, the wounds on the skulls suggested that those people could have died due to blows to their necks, shoulders and the back of their heads by big, round objects – like *hailstones*.

There are many theories about whom the skeletons belong to – they could be locals, pilgrims, traders or even army men. But until the truth is uncovered, the story that at least one set of skeletons belong to Jasdhaval, Balampha and their troupe of entertainers will continue to haunt Roopkund's waters.

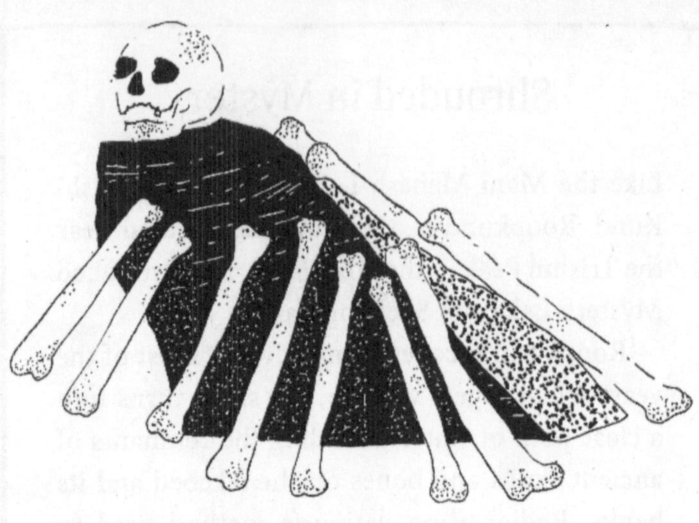

Goddess Nanda Devi reduced erring devotees to mere skeletons. But did you know that a hill tribe once hosted a goddess who was nothing more than skin and bones herself?

14

The Gift of a Hungry Goddess

Khandadhar

'I'm still hungry!' the goddess's voice boomed.

'What do we do now? There's nothing left to give her – except our own homes,' a worried man cried out. The group of people looked at each other helplessly.

'But the goddess must be fed!' an old woman said.

'Oh! What if we take her to the mountaintop?' a little girl suggested, pointing towards the huge mountains that overlooked their homes.

The Pauri Bhuiyan people lived in a forested terrain. Reddish-black earth carpeted the region, and large, sculpted mountains stood around it. Mainly farmers, the Pauri Bhuiyans moved and changed their farms every few years. Sometimes, it was a challenge to find a good patch of cultivable land. It was also equally difficult to find water sources nearby to irrigate their farms and take care of their daily needs. But the Pauri Bhuiyans didn't complain. They led a simple life with whatever means they had.

One day, a goddess named Kankala Devi appeared in the region. The people froze when they saw her. More than her sudden appearance, it was her unusual frame that shocked them.

'What's this? The goddess looks *famished*,' an old woman whispered.

Kankala Devi's eyes were sunk deep into their sockets. There were dents where her cheeks should have been. Her hands, fingers, feet and toes, all looked like they were only bones, with no skin on them.

'Will you feed me?' she asked them, her voice weak and barely audible. The courteous and good-hearted Pauri Bhuiyans immediately agreed.

But they soon realized that this was no easy task. No food that they offered her from their modest homes could satiate her enormous appetite. As they scrounged for more food, Kankala Devi asked, 'Can I eat these?' pointing to all the vegetation around.

The people stood speechless, but the old woman spoke up again, 'As you please, Goddess!' Kankala Devi began uprooting trees and devouring them whole.

The stunned group stepped back and watched her gobble up tree after tree, plant after plant, and shrub after shrub. The land was cleared of all its green cover!

'I'm ravenous,' the goddess declared, shrugging at the increasingly alarmed Pauri Bhuiyans.

Again, they offered her whatever little they had left with them, but Kankala Devi's hunger only grew. 'Can I eat those?' she asked, pointing at the ground.

The people nodded. So she began eating the stones and pebbles around, and even the soil! The hungry goddess just couldn't help herself, and went on eating, chewing and swallowing parts of the land.

When she had scraped off a whole layer of the ground, she told her amazed audience, 'Stomach's growling again. What else can I eat?'

That's when a little girl suggested that they should perhaps take her up to the mountains.

'Kankala Devi, we offer you these mountains! Take your seat on this range. You'll surely find a lot to eat here,' said the old woman.

'So much food!' the goddess exclaimed as she sat on the peak of one of the mountains and looked around. Hungrily, she bit into a large chunk of the mountain and swallowed it.

The people continued to watch her from a distance, holding their breath. A gaping hole now stared back at them instead of the peak.

Finally, with a look of satisfaction, Kankala Devi smiled. 'You've fed me well. Now, it's my turn to give you something.'

As soon as she had spoken these words, a milky white stream began flowing down from the broken crown of the mountain.

'Water!' a man yelled.

The tribespeople were overjoyed.

Ever since, all the water needs of the Pauri Bhuiyans have been fulfilled by this cascading stream. They didn't have to worry about water anymore and could go about their everyday life with ease.

And oh, they could grow many, many varieties of crops too!

Connecting the Dots...

An endangered community who live in Odisha, the Pauri Bhuiyan people get their name and identity from the landscape they inhabit – pauri *comes from the word* pahari, *which means 'hill' or 'mountain', while* bhuiyan *has its roots in* bhumi, *which means 'earth' or 'land'. The Pauri Bhuiyans believe that the hills and the forests belong to them as much as the tribe belongs to the land.*

The community is known to practise shifting cultivation, a farming method in which they clear a patch of the forest and turn it into farmland for a few years. Once they use it well, they discard it, find another piece of land and repeat the process until the first one becomes fertile again. The waterfall that Kankala Devi gifted the Pauri Bhuiyans is called the Khandadhar Falls, and it is located in the Khandadhar Mountain Range in the Sundargarh district of Odisha.

While one legend suggests that the hungry goddess who visited the land of the Pauri Bhuiyans was Kankala Devi, another legend says that it is the goddess Kanta Devi (also called Kanteshwari, Kanta Kumari or Khanda Kumari) who resides in the Khandadhar Mountain Range and who gave them the bounty of nature.

A Tale of Two Falls

Khandadhar gets its name from the words *khanda* or 'sword' and *dhara* or 'waterfall', meaning the 'waterfall that is shaped like a sword'. Interestingly, there are two waterfalls by the name of Khandadhar in Odisha. Situated on either side of the Khandadhar Range, one lies in the Sundargarh district, while the other is in the neighbouring district of Keonjhar or Kendujhar. This is because a stream called Korapani Nala, which flows through the Khandadhar Mountains, cascades as the Khandadhar Falls in both these districts.

The Terrible Soil Eater

Flowing down from a height of 800 feet, the Khandadhar Falls in Sundargarh is the highest waterfall in Odisha and the twelfth highest in India. When a waterbody flows over a series of hard and soft rocks, it erodes the soft rocks over time. These break away, leaving a gaping or ledge-like hard rock on the edge of a hill or mountain, from which the waterbody then plunges down and creates a pool of water below. This cascading stream is called a waterfall.

The Khandadhar Falls provide water to several villages in Sundargarh and Keonjhar through the rivers Baitarni and Brahmani. But in recent years, parts of the waterfall have been drying up, and the volume of water flowing into these two rivers has reduced drastically. The water running through the Pauri Bhuiyan farms has been red in colour, especially during the monsoon – this is because the reddish-black soil in the region has loosened, and it mixes with the flowing water. And so, the crops in the fields as well as the fish in the rivers have been dying.

No, Kankala Devi is not chomping on these again! This time, the big eater is the mining industry. The reddish-black earth of the Khandadhar region gets its colour from the iron ore deposits it contains. Excessive mining has destroyed the forests, dried up the Khandadhar Falls, polluted the waterbodies with the loose soil and mining waste, and covered the region in red dust.

As a result, the Pauri Bhuiyan community, whose beliefs and lifestyle are closely linked with the waterfall, is in danger as well. These forest dwellers have been asked to shift away from their lands so they can be mined. Many have been forced to quit farming due to the non-availability of land and water. Left with no other choice, some have become workers in the very local mines that have changed their lives.

The tribespeople had readily offered the mountains to the hungry goddess, but they would never feed their land to greedy individuals who wish to devour its mineral resources.

The Endangered Guardians

India's indigenous people are called adivasis, a term that means 'earliest inhabitants'. The Pauri Bhuiyan is one such tribe. Some anthropologists say that they are genetically similar to the Great Andamanese, Jarawa and Onge tribes of the Andaman Islands, and that they have inhabited the earth for 24 millennia!

The Pauri Bhuiyan consider themselves to be the owners and protectors of the land. They coat the walls of their homes with the reddish-black soil, and even use earthen utensils. So high is their regard for the earth that they touch it or hold a fistful of soil when taking an oath.

With the land falling apart, their legends, customs, and survival itself are at risk. They now feature on the country's list of Particularly Vulnerable Tribal Groups.

Kankala Devi chose the land and the people she wanted to watch over. But did you know that there was a goddess who left this decision to her father?

15

A Water Kingdom for a Princess

Loktak

The king of Sana Leibak had always known that his seventh daughter was different – right from the time he had first held her in his arms, when she was born.

'She looks so calm…so unlike our other girls,' the king had told the queen then.

As a child, while her sisters fought over trivial matters, the princess would just watch them quietly. Her sisters demanded to be treated like princesses, but the youngest one was always polite and humble.

Pushing these thoughts aside, the king focused on the present problem. The princess, who had grown into a fine young lady, had asked him to take an important decision for her. 'What do I do now?' he wondered. All that came to his mind were the princess's kind eyes and gentle smile.

'Yes!' he exclaimed suddenly. 'I've got it! *That* is the perfect gift for her!'

A few days ago, the king of Sana Leibak had called an official meeting with his seven daughters.

'What's the matter, Father? Are you organizing a feast?' the eldest princess asked as all of them walked in together and sat around him.

'No, dear,' he said, smiling. 'I've been thinking...I feel that the time has come for me to pass on the reins of the kingdom to your hands.'

'That's a great decision!' his second daughter said.

'You should retire now, Father,' said the third, and the fourth added, 'Yes, we'll manage the kingdom, don't you worry!'

'My princesses are capable of leading the land and its people, I'm sure of that,' he said.

'Oh, but how can all of us rule the same kingdom together?' the fifth daughter asked.

'You're right,' the king said. 'That's why I've decided that each of you will rule over a separate region.'

'Great! I hope we get to pick the place we want, because I have already thought of where I would like to live,' the sixth princess said.

'Hmm,' the king said and nodded quietly.

The young girls were thrilled. They whispered furiously to each other, discussing their preferences. The seventh and youngest daughter only listened.

'Are all of you ready with the names of the places?' the king asked, clearing his throat.

One by one, the princesses announced their choices.

'Given! Done! As you wish, my dear!' The king officially granted them control over the regions they'd named. 'And what about you, little one?' he asked the youngest.

'As *you* wish, Father!' she answered.

'Don't you want to pick a place for yourself like your sisters have?' he asked her.

'Think of a place you really like,' her eldest sister suggested.

'I like all the places in the kingdom equally,' the young princess said. 'I'll be happy if you chose a region for me, Father. You know me and this land well.'

The king was touched to see that his daughter trusted his judgement and wisdom. But he now had the responsibility of making a fair decision on her behalf.

After a whole week of contemplation, the king told the youngest princess, 'I've finally chosen a kingdom for you, my dear.' The other daughters looked on, wondering what their father would say.

'Loktak Pat!' the beaming king exclaimed. 'At first, it was difficult to find a suitable place for you, little one. But when I thought of your kind eyes and smile, it reminded me of the serene waters of Loktak.'

'Thank you, Father!' she said, smiling radiantly.

And so, the seven princesses went to live in their own new kingdoms. The people of Loktak were so much in awe of the youngest princess's compassion that they began calling her Loktak Lairembee, or the 'goddess of Loktak'!

Connecting the Dots...

Sana Leibak, which means 'land of gold', is one of the ancient names of Manipur. Loktak Pat is a placid freshwater lake situated in a town called Moirang in Manipur. People from the Meitei community (an indigenous group of people from the state) believe that the lake is their lairembee *or 'goddess', and that she looks after them like a mother. They respect her waters like her children and also refer to her as* Ima Lairembee, *meaning 'mother goddess'.*

A Floating World

The name Loktak comes from two Manipuri words: *lok*, which means 'stream', and *tak*, which means 'end'. As many as 42 rivers and rivulets flow into Loktak, thus making it the place where the streams end. The word *pat*, in Manipuri, means 'lake'. Loktak is the largest freshwater lake in north-east India. Referred to as the lifeline of Manipur, it caters to the basic water and electricity needs of the state's people, especially those who live around it.

Loktak Lake is best known for the *phumdi*s that have formed over its waters. *Phumdi* is the Manipuri word for a floating mat made up of vegetation (often tangled roots and stems), soil, decaying plants and other organic matter. It moves about on the surface of the lake, depending on the water levels.

The lower portion of a *phumdi* stays underwater. During the dry season, as the water level goes down, the *phumdi* descends with it, right to the bottom of the lakebed. When this happens, the roots connect with and absorb the required nutrients from the soil of the lake floor. During the monsoon, when the water levels go up, the *phumdi* rises up again, completely rejuvenated!

Another fascinating aspect of Loktak is the unique fishing technique practised there by the locals. In this method, strips of *phumdi*s are first cut and arranged on the surface of the lake in the shape of a ring. Then, certain plant species which attract fish are placed in the circular ponds that are enclosed by these ring-like *phumdi*s.

When viewed from the top, Loktak looks like a drawing sheet on which the people have practised reproducing the geometric shape many times, as its vast expanse is patterned with several such circular green strips.

The Dance of the Sangai

On the southern side of the lake is its largest *phumdi,* over which the world's only floating wildlife reserve, the Keibul Lamjao National Park, is situated. The highlight of the park is the Sangai deer, a species found exclusively near Loktak Lake. The Sangai are famously known as 'dancing deer' because the way they walk and balance themselves on the floating swamps makes them appear like they are dancing! Sadly, the slow destruction of this animal's only natural habitat has endangered the species.

Keeping Meitei Roots Afloat

Many people have made Loktak their home – some reside on the banks of the lake, and others on its islands. But one of the most amazing things about the lake is that an entire community (mostly the Meitei fisherfolk) has been living in thatched homes built over the lake's *phumdis*. Imagine having homes that are often on the move! In recent times though, living on *phumdis* has been discouraged, due to the damage caused to this unique ecosystem by human habitation.

However, conservationists as well as locals believe that the lake and the *phumdis* have been affected by the construction of the Ithai Barrage. This dam was built a few years ago to harness the Loktak Lake's waters for irrigation and hydroelectricity (the electrical power produced by moving or flowing water). With so many rivers flowing into the lake, and the barrage

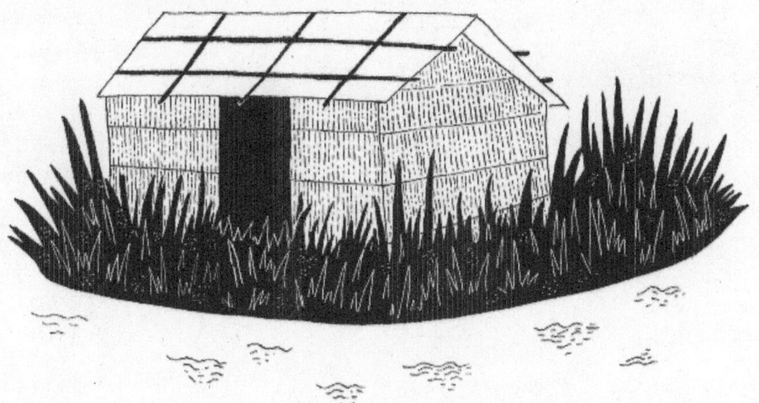

preventing the waters from flowing out, the lake's water levels are high in all seasons and have begun to destroy the *phumdis*.

Since the water level doesn't go down even in the dry season, the *phumdis* can no longer descend to the lakebed and regain their health by soaking in nutrients from the soil. As a result, more and more vegetation has begun to decay and remain inside the lake's waters.

These unusual floating islands exist only on Loktak Lake and cannot be found anywhere else in the world. It would be a true loss if the *phumdis* continue to decay and reduce in size and number. The foods, festivals, beliefs, folklore and boat races held on the lake, along with many other aspects of Manipuri life, especially Meitei culture, are at risk of dying too.

Just as the king had faith in his youngest daughter, the Meitei people's hopes are pinned on Loktak Lairembee now. Will she succeed in protecting the region all by herself?

In Royal Realms

Like the gods and indigenous tribes, ancient kings and queens too shared a special relationship with the landscape around their kingdoms and the places they travelled through.

But, being powerful royals who possibly believed that they could control everything and everyone, how did they react to the surprises that nature threw at them?

16

A King Lost, a Land Found

Bangaram

Loud laughter echoed through the royal hall. Cheraman Perumal was in awe of how well travelled his guests were. In fact, it was to find out more about distant places and people's lifestyles elsewhere that he had invited these Arab merchants, who were passing through his kingdom, to a royal feast.

As the food and conversation flowed, one of the merchants exclaimed, 'The moon looks so mesmerizing! Almost reminds me of that night some months ago, when the moon miracle occurred!'

Cheraman Perumal sat upright on hearing these words. 'Moon miracle?'

'Yes, the one caused by the Prophet,' the merchant said. 'Prophet Muhammad. He lives in Mecca,' he added.

Cheraman Perumal had heard this name for the first time. But he could not stop thinking about the miracle man after that day. Early one morning, he called his minister and said, 'I'm going on a quest soon, but keep this a secret!'

A few months ago, Cheraman Perumal, the ruler of the great Chera dynasty, had been enjoying a post-dinner walk on the spacious porch outside his chamber. A big, luminous moon caught his attention. As he stood admiring it, something strange occurred.

'It can't be!' the king exclaimed, rubbing his eyes in disbelief.

The full moon that he had been gazing at had suddenly split into two globes! Cheraman Perumal looked around to check if anyone else could also see the two moons. But before he could call one of his guards, the two moons merged back into one again. The king stared at the sky for a very long time, but nothing else happened. He couldn't sleep that night. Curiosity and excitement kept him awake.

The next morning, the king asked to see the royal astrologer. As soon as the astrologer came in and took his seat, the king impatiently plied him with questions. 'What I saw last night – the moon splitting into two and fusing back – was it my imagination?'

'No, it did happen,' the astrologer said gravely. 'But I believe very few were lucky to have witnessed this miracle.'

'How did it happen? And why?' the king asked.

'All I can say is that it could be a sign. And that you will find your answers soon.'

Over the next few weeks, Cheraman Perumal consulted many other astrologers, and they all told him the same thing – that it could be a sign. But no one was willing to say any more. The king was sure that the astrologers were hiding something from him.

Finally, it was the Arab merchants he had invited to a feast who inadvertently told him who had caused the supernatural event: Prophet Muhammad. Cheraman Perumal felt a yearning to meet and learn from the Prophet. *If he performs miracles, he is surely a wise man*, the king thought. He understood that this was the sign all the astrologers had spoken about. They didn't tell him more because they foresaw what he would do once he heard about the miracle man.

Sure enough, the king told his minister about his plans to quietly leave the kingdom. 'It's best I abdicate the throne, before embarking on this journey. I don't know if I will ever come back.' He had his will prepared, with detailed notes on how his kingdom was to be divided and who would rule over which parts.

Yet, when the news of Cheraman Perumal's disappearance reached the kings of the neighbouring kingdoms, they were worried about what this meant for them and the security of their territories.

'We must find Cheraman Perumal and bring him back,' the raja of Cannanore said to his commander. 'The rulers of the other neighbouring regions are sending out search parties to find him. We should also send out a group of soldiers immediately!'

'What if Cheraman Perumal has taken the sea route?' the commander asked.

And so, a search party sailed from the harbour of Cannanore. But on the way, the ship with the troops on board was caught in a terrible storm, and it crashed onto an isolated island. The marooned soldiers had no choice but to spend a few days there, and they managed to survive on the fish they caught. At last, they made their way back to Cannanore on a rescue ship. During their return journey, the soldiers found many such uninhabited islands in the sea.

When they reached Cannanore, they reported their adventures to the raja, who became upset, fearing that Cheraman Perumal's ship had met the same fate as that of his soldiers.

'Alas, a king is lost,' he said to himself sadly.

However, days later, another group of soldiers, along with their families, was sent out to explore and settle on the unknown islands dotting the sea.

'But what do we do there?' a soldier asked the raja.

'Why, it's in the middle of so much water. Cultivate coconut plantations, take up fishing!' said the raja.

So, this time, when the troops discovered yet another island, they began building a new life there by doing what the raja had suggested – growing coconuts and catching fish.

Meanwhile, unbeknownst to the raja of Cannanore and the other rulers of the region, Cheraman Perumal had travelled all the way to Mecca.

There, he met Prophet Muhammad, the messenger of Allah (the all-powerful god in Islam), who was spreading the message of the faith. Cheraman Perumal was greatly inspired by the Prophet and his teachings. He adopted Islam as a new way of life and stayed in Mecca for a few years.

But, one day, he told the Prophet, 'It's time for me to go back to my kingdom. I'm taking your teachings with me.'

Cheraman Perumal began his homeward journey. As he made his way back, he preached Islam to people in different places along the route. But somewhere along the journey, he fell seriously ill.

'I don't think I will see the Chera kingdom again,' he said to Malik bin Dinar, a friend who was travelling with him. 'Take these letters to the rulers of my region and tell them that it is Cheraman Perumal's final wish that Islam lives on in his kingdom.'

After the king passed away, Malik travelled along with his family and companions to the Chera kingdom. They not only spread the teachings of Islam, but also built many Islamic shrines across the region. By fulfilling Cheraman Perumal's last wish, they had completed his quest.

Connecting the Dots...

Cheraman Perumal was not this particular king's name. It was, in fact, the title given to the kings of the Chera dynasty. In Malayalam and Tamil, the word perumal *means 'great being' or 'god'. Since the people of this region saw their kings as almost equal to gods, the title 'Cheraman Perumal' was bestowed upon the kings. Similarly, raja,* kolathiri *or* kolathiri *raja were titles given to the leaders or heads of certain regions in Kerala at that time, and the raja of Cannanore was one of them.*

The Cannanore troops who went looking for Cheraman Perumal discovered the islands in the archipelago of Lakshadweep in the Arabian Sea. It is believed that the troops began living on some of these islands, and this population slowly spread to neighbouring islands. The main occupations of the island's inhabitants were coconut cultivation and fishing, which are practised there even today. On the other hand, the island where the troops were shipwrecked is still among the few uninhabited places of Lakshadweep – it is known today as Bangaram.

Cheraman's Masjid

There is a mosque in Kodungallur in Kerala, built as early as the seventh century, that is dedicated to Cheraman Perumal. Kodungallur was earlier known as Cranganore, and was the capital of Cheraman Perumal's kingdom. The Cheraman Juma Masjid, as the mosque is called, is believed to be the oldest mosque in India. It was one of the many shrines built by Malik bin Dinar and his companions.

A Mountain in the Sea

A group of unconnected, separate islands in a sea is known as an archipelago. Lakshadweep is an archipelago, and its name stems from the belief that it is made up of one lakh islands. In reality, Lakshadweep consists of 10 inhabited islands, 17 uninhabited islands (along with their islets), 4 newly formed islets, 12 atolls, 3 reefs and 5 submerged banks.

Lakshadweep lies scattered across the Arabian Sea, off the south-western coast of India. It is one of the three archipelagos that form the Laccadive–Chagos Ridge, the other two archipelagos being the Maldives Ridge and the Chagos Bank. The Laccadive–Chagos Ridge is actually an underwater volcanic mountain range, believed to be the submerged extension of the Aravalli Range of Rajasthan. The ridge is said to have been formed by a chain of underwater volcanoes.

Only the mountaintops along the ridge are visible above the water surface at various places between the Arabian Sea and the Indian Ocean as the Lakshadweep, Maldives, and Chagos group of islands. Lakshadweep, in the Arabian Sea, is the northernmost of the three archipelagos; Maldives is in between; Chagos lies to the south, closer to the Indian Ocean.

The Colourful Circle of Life

Corals are colourful aquatic animals – no, they aren't plants, even though they look like colourful shrubs. The larvae of corals often attach themselves to the seabed, underwater rocks and the edges of volcanic islands. When a volcano erupts underwater and the lava eventually cools over it, a new crest is formed. As only the crest is visible above the water, it looks like an island. This is called a volcanic island.

Water erodes the surface of such islands continuously. Over time, the visible top of the volcanic island slowly decreases in height due to this erosion, and is finally submerged. In the meantime, corals grow in clusters or colonies along the island's edges, forming coral banks or reefs. By the time the island is completely submerged, the corals around its perimeter grow so large that they become visible through or above the water's surface. When the area where the island once stood gets covered by water, only the ring of colourful corals is seen around it. Such submerged islands with ring-shaped reefs and a lagoon in the centre are called atolls.

Corals take thousands of years to grow into a reef, while an atoll can take lakhs of years to form. Bangaram Atoll, which is part of Lakshadweep as well as the Laccadive–Chagos Ridge, has also evolved this way. The Laccadive–Chagos Ridge is the world's largest atoll ecosystem.

Both coral reefs and atolls prevent erosion and provide shelter and food to many aquatic species. They are also important sources of life-saving medicines.

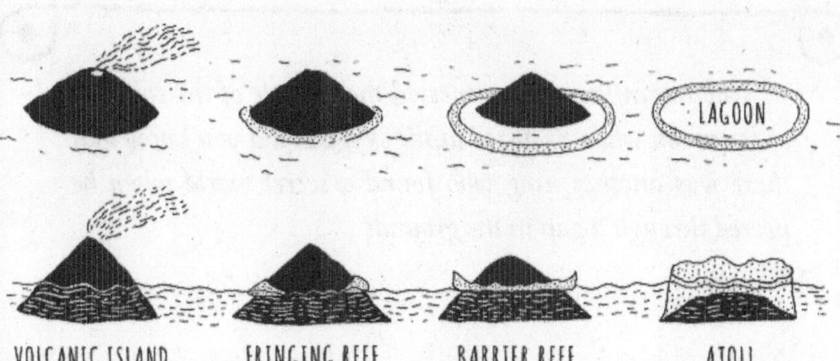

Hide-and-Seek

With the volcanic island disappearing into the sea and the coral reef appearing above the water surface, atolls such as Bangaram seem to be constantly playing hide-and-seek. But this game of nature is being ruined by human players.

Earlier, Bangaram Atoll was made up of five islands – Bangaram, Thinnakara, Parali 1, Parali 2 and Parali 3. Conservationists have found that Parali 1 has entirely disappeared due to climate change and erosion. The ecosystems in the other islands of Lakshadweep are also disintegrating due to human activities such as the clearing of reefs for coconut plantations, construction on the delicate lands for tourism, and coral mining.

And so, environmentalists are doing their best to make sure the country's rich atoll system does not vanish entirely from the world map.

Cheraman Perumal witnessed the miracle of the splitting of the moon when he gazed at the sky. But did you know that there was another king who found a secret world when he peered through a gap in the ground?

17

A Cave of Wonders

Patal Bhuvaneshwar

Raja Rituparna cautiously peered into the hole in the rocks that he had stumbled upon. He had expected the secret cave behind the hole to hold all sorts of things – a trove of hidden treasure, an enemy hideout, or even a demon's lair!

But in the darkness of the cave, Raja Rituparna could only see two beady, glowing eyes staring back at him. They seemed to be slowly gliding towards him, but the king was so awestruck that he could hardly move. And then, the most wondrous thing happened!

Once, Raja Rituparna was sauntering through the thick forests that surrounded his kingdom. Although he had been to this region many times before, he usually ended up discovering an uncharted path or area on every visit.

Suddenly, he saw a flash of gold. 'Oh! What a strange-looking deer!' he exclaimed, and began following the glowing animal. But somewhere along the way, he lost track of it. Tired by then – for he had been travelling for a while – he fell asleep beneath a tall pine tree.

'Don't chase me,' the deer said to the king, appearing in his dream. 'I'm not really a deer.'

Rituparna woke up with a start. He looked around and realized that he had never been to this part of the woods before.

'Wait, what's that hole?' he said to himself, spotting a small opening near some rocks.

'It doesn't look like an animal's burrow,' he muttered. As he went close to it, he suddenly saw a demon with horns and a golden aura – somehow, he reminded the king of the strange-looking deer. But the magical creature vanished on seeing him.

That's when the king noticed the yaksha, a divine spirit, who was keeping watch right outside the hole. *If such a small opening is being guarded by a yaksha, there's surely someone or something important inside. But who or what is it?* he wondered as he approached the guard.

'Ahem... I'm Raja Rituparna. I wish to see what's inside,' he said to the yaksha, pointing to the gap in the rocks.

'Till *our* king agrees, I can't let you go in,' replied the spirit.

Rituparna was now very curious. He requested the yaksha to let him pass again, but the latter refused. The king then firmly ordered the yaksha to let him in. That didn't work either. Finally, he resorted to pleas.

'All right, I shall inform our king about your request,' the divine spirit said, going into the hole, only to return a few moments later and say, 'he is ready to meet you.'

Rituparna was thrilled. As he peered into the hole, he was greeted by a pair of glowing eyes. The king of the cave then came closer and revealed himself. Rituparna was taken aback to see that he was not human.

'Easy, friend,' said the king of the cave, and stuck out his large serpent head. 'Greetings! I am Sheshnag.'

Rituparna rubbed his eyes, but this was no dream. '*Sh-Shesh-nag* – the king of serpents? The one with a thousand heads? The one who holds the planets and the universe on his hoods? The one who…'

'Whoa-whoa-whoa! Hold on. Yes, that's all me!' the serpent grinned, revealing giant fangs.

Raja Rituparna blinked. 'Well, what are you doing *here*?'

'Guarding the hidden world of thirty-three crore gods, of course! Would you like to see *my* Patal?' Sheshnag asked.

'Patal?' Raja Rituparna's jaw dropped. Just as he was about to enter the cave, the serpent king cautioned him, 'Careful! It's steep in here – a straight drop from the hole, several feet down. No steps, so that humans can't enter easily. Why don't you leap onto one of my hoods? I'll take you around.'

Sheshnag retreated into the hole and positioned himself in a way that the king could easily land on his head, without losing his balance.

Rituparna gulped. From the edge of the hole, as he peeped in, it was indeed a direct drop. He inhaled, and took the leap of faith, landing perfectly on Sheshnag's head.

'Who would imagine your thousand heads would fit into such a small opening?' Rituparna marvelled, settling comfortably on one of Sheshnag's hoods.

'We snakes can make our way through all kinds of gaps and holes,' Sheshnag said.

And so, with the divine being as his guide, Raja Rituparna began his grand tour of the cave. From his privileged seat, he had a fantastic view.

'Where are the thirty-three crore gods?' Raja Rituparna asked, his excitement increasing by the second.

'They're all here. There! That's Adi Ganesha's severed head. Do you see the inverted lotus above it? Well, that flower sprinkled amrit – the nectar of immortality – over Ganesha's severed head and his headless form, until Shiva gave him an elephant head and revived him.

'Oh, by the way, meet Goddess Bhuvaneshwari,' Sheshnag added, as he glided past the goddess.

Rituparna joined his hands to seek her blessings.

'What's this? A swan? Why is its head turned the other way?' Rituparna asked, distracted by an odd-looking bird a little ahead.

'Ah, you see those seven tiny ponds? Those belong to the gods, and they are filled with amrit. The swan was supposed to guard the amrit, but it tasted some instead one day. So, it has been cursed to look away from the seven pools of amrit forever!' Sheshnag explained.

'Oh!' Rituparna shook his head in disappointment. Suddenly, something in the distance that looked white, black and brown caught his attention. 'What's that? It covers the full length of the cave's wall!'

'*Sshh*...the lord is meditating. Those are Shiva's tresses. The white part, I'm sure you know, is Goddess Ganga flowing from his locks as a stream,' Sheshnag said, bowing to them before moving ahead.

'That is the Vishwakarma Kund,' the giant serpent said, stopping near a tank next. 'It is named after the divine architect of the world of the gods, as he created this pool of water too. See the impression of his hand? Behind it are Brahma, Vishnu and Shiva. And to the side are the other thirty-three crore gods!'

Rituparna was so mesmerized that he didn't even realize that Shiva appeared at once in multiple places around the cave.

Sheshnag then showed the king three more paths tunnelling further ahead into the cave. 'One leads to Kailash Mansarovar – Shiva's abode, another to Swarga – that's paradise, and the last one goes to the holy town of Badrinath.'

'So, which tunnel are we going through first?' Rituparna asked.

Sheshnag shook his hoods lightly and said, 'No, friend. I can't take you any further.'

With that, Sheshnag ended Rituparna's awe-inspiring journey and brought him back to the cave entrance.

'Thank you, Sheshnag,' Rituparna said, overwhelmed. 'I will cherish this meeting and the tour around your Patal forever!'

'My pleasure! But promise me, friend,' Sheshnag warned, 'not a word about this to anyone!'

'I promise!' the king said as he left for his palace. He was truly happy – he felt privileged to have seen Sheshnag's secret world.

Back home, Rituparna's queen, who had been anxiously waiting for him, was relieved to see him. 'Where have you been? What took you so long? I even sent out a search party, but no one could find you!'

'Relax, relax. I was just chasing a deer,' the king said.

'So where is it then?' the queen asked.

'No, I mean, I was chasing a deer in my dream. But uh, it wasn't a deer at all,' the king blurted out, struggling to lie to his dear wife.

'A deer that wasn't a deer? What was it then?' she pestered.

'I don't know what it was, maybe it was a spirit or something...' he said uncertainly, turning away.

'What on earth are you talking about?' she asked suspiciously. 'It's clear you're hiding something from me!'

Unable to contain his excitement any longer, Rituparna told her everything.

'I want to see them too!' the queen exclaimed. The king begged her not to go, reminding her of his promise to Sheshnag. But the queen wouldn't listen.

'If he was so nice to you, I'm sure he wouldn't mind a visit from me,' she said and began making preparations for her journey to the woods.

But when she reached the cave, she found no deer or spirit. Sheshnag didn't come out to welcome her either. So, the queen used a rope to enter the cave. Needless to say, she was most upset by what she saw inside – the marvellous sights that Raja Rituparna had gushed about had vanished!

No gods sat there now. Instead, only rock and stone formations that resembled the divine beings were left behind. The king had, after all, broken his promise to Sheshnag.

Connecting the Dots...

Raja Rituparna is believed to have discovered and toured the Patal Bhuvaneshwar Cave, which lies in Uttarakhand's Pithoragarh district. Some say that the cave is named after the idol of Goddess Bhuvaneshwari found inside it, while others suggest that the cave gets its name from Shiva, who resided and meditated there, for he is also known as Bhuvaneshwar ('lord of the world').

Today, there are several rock-cut steps that lead people into the cave where humans were once allowed no entry. As soon as they reach the base of the cave, the hood and fangs of Sheshnag are visible in their rocky form, as the cave's ceiling. People believe this proves that the serpent king had indeed transformed himself into the tunnel-like cave at the very place where his hidden world existed, after Rituparna broke his promise.

So, when they travel through the cave to see the rock formations (which resemble the divine beings and objects that Raja Rituparna had seen), they believe that they are actually walking through the winding form (especially the spine) of the divine snake.

The Chamber of Secrets

According to Indian mythology, Patal Lok is situated below Prithvi Lok and is made up of seven realms, or worlds, that are located one below the other. The lowermost among these is Naga Lok, the world of snakes.

Tales of iconic snakes from Indian mythology continue to echo through the chambers of Patal Bhuvaneshwar. A hole in the floor is connected to the legend of the serpent Takshak and King Janmajeya, who performed a yajna to sacrifice all snakes, even the ones living in Patal Lok. A rope-like rocky form jutting out of the cave's wall tells the story of Vasuki, the serpent who was used as a rope around Mount Meru, to churn the ocean of milk and extract amrit for the gods and asuras. And Sheshavati, a rugged chamber inside Patal Bhuvaneshwar, is believed to be the abode of *ichchhadari nag* and *naagin*, shape-shifting cobras that can mysteriously change their form at will and appear as human beings.

The Magic of Minerals

Caves are underground cavities or chambers that form naturally in the bedrock (the solid rock below the earth's surface) because of the melting of ice (from glaciers nearby), volcanic activity, tectonic movement, or the action of water on the rock. The most common are caves formed by groundwater activity on limestone bedrocks.

Patal Bhuvaneshwar is a tunnel-like chain of connected limestone caves known for its speleothems. These are formations inside caves that are created over the course of hundreds of years by the action of water and its minerals on the cave's surfaces. Found on the ceiling, ground and walls of a cave, these formations are of various shapes, sizes and colours. There are many types of speleothems – stalagmite, stalactite, flowstone, column, soda straw and so on.

Stalagmites protrude from the ground inside a cave, while stalactites hang from the ceiling. A stalactite usually has a stalagmite forming right below it, as they occur in pairs. The water dripping from the ceiling causes a stalactite to hang from it. When some of the water drips or falls on the ground right below it, a stalagmite is formed on the floor of the cave. In geological terms, the rocky element that resembles the severed head of Ganesha at Patal Bhuvaneshwar is a stalagmite, and the inverted lotus above it is a stalactite.

Similarly, the wrinkled, rocky ground of the cave, which resembles the spine or the scaly belly of a giant snake, has also been caused by the action of water.

The Speleothem Spectrum

Not all caves and their rocky formations are brown. The colour of the speleothems depends on the mineral content in the water.

The presence of the mineral calcite can cause white formations, while that of iron can lead to red, orange, brown and black formations. So the white, brown and black object covering a large part of a wall in the Patal Bhuvaneshwar Cave looked like Shiva's tresses to Sheshnag and Raja Rituparna. But to geologists, it is primarily a multicoloured speleothem formed by a combination of minerals in the water!

The world of gods that Raja Rituparna had toured was turned into a rocky cave because the king didn't keep his word. But did you know that there was another king who received a divine present for his upright nature?

18

An Honest King's Reward

Sambhar

'I want to give you something for your goodness,' the *vidyadhara* said to Vasudeva. 'Ah, yes! I know! Kind king, strike the ground here with your sword and begin riding towards your capital. But remember, no matter what happens, don't look back.' With these words, the *vidyadhara* vanished into silvery dust.

Vasudeva tried to replay the words that the *vidyadhara* had spoken in his mind. He was used to the fast-talking divine being by now, but he still needed time to register all that he had said.

'All right,' Vasudeva said, sitting comfortably on his horse. After striking the ground with his sword, he rode for a while. But, at one point, he began hearing the sound of waves behind him. *Shhooooshh...swooooshhh... shhhooshhhh...*

What's going on? Sounds like an entire ocean is following me, and it seems like it might drown me any moment, Vasudeva thought. Worried, he turned his head to look.

'What a great day of hunting!' said King Vasudeva, patting his horse. Luck had favoured him even though he was far from the capital of his kingdom, in a region he hadn't known of before.

'Hmm, I like this place. I think we should build a palace here. What say, friend?' he asked his horse, who grunted in response. Vasudeva laughed and said, 'I take that as a "yes"!'

The most splendid palace was constructed in this newly discovered place. When it was ready, Vasudeva turned it into a retreat. 'No one except me should be allowed to enter this palace,' he told the guards.

But one afternoon, when Vasudeva returned to his palace after yet another day of successful hunting, he noticed that the windows of his chambers were wide open. He entered cautiously, holding his sword firmly in one hand.

As he surveyed the room, he was most amused to find a stranger asleep on his royal bed. '*Khhrrr… khurrrr...khrrrr...khuurrr…*' the stranger snored. The king smiled, putting his sword back into its sheath. Just then, something fell out of the stranger's half-open mouth and rolled towards Vasudeva.

'What's this?' the king wondered as he picked it up. The thing glowed against the early evening light of the sun filtering in through the open window. 'A magical pill! Oh my, the stranger is a *vidyadhara*!' he exclaimed.

Vasudeva knew that *vidyadhara*s were wise, divine beings, believed to be holders of knowledge – in fact, they got their name from the Sanskrit words *vidya*, meaning 'knowledge', and *dhara*, meaning 'holder'. But what he found most fascinating about them was that they could fly.

He was thrilled to notice that the stranger in his room had wings! 'Wow!' he exclaimed.

Startled by Vasudeva's voice, the stranger woke up and immediately leapt towards the open window, hoping to escape. But he fell flat on the ground. '*Oww*, my beautiful chin! I think I've broken it!'

The king laughed and helped him up. 'Here, you might need this if you want to fly out of that window,' he told the stranger, handing him the magical pill. 'You're a *vidyadhara*, right?'

'Goddess Shakambhari be blessed, I have never met such a truthful being!' the stranger exclaimed, and hugged the king. 'I was fast asleep. You know who I am, you know what that pill is used for, and you *still* didn't steal it and use it to fly away!' he said in wonder.

'Well, you are a *vidyadhara*, you need this pill. I'm just a king, I don't need to fly. My horse is good enough for me,' Vasudeva said modestly.

The *vidyadhara* blinked at the king in disbelief. 'I'm the son of the *vidyadhara* Shakambhara, who is a great devotee of Goddess Shakambhari. Do you know the goddess was so impressed by my father's penance that she now resides in this region, in a shrine a short distance from here? I go there often. I was returning from there today when I saw your beautiful palace. I just wanted to have a quick look. But then I saw your beautiful bed, and I immediately wanted to lie down on it. I did, and it was so cosy I fell asleep… Wait, was I snoring?' he asked, looking worried.

Before the smiling king could respond, the *vidyadhara* prattled on non-stop, 'Goddess Shakambhari be blessed! I must do something for you. But what? You already have so much wealth. You have a prosperous kingdom. Your children and their children will have all they ever need. Oh wait, I know what! Ask your guards and your soldiers to go back to your capital.'

'What? But…' the king began.

'Come on, king, just do as I say. Oh, what's your name by the way? Never mind. It's almost time for sunset. Quick!'

Vasudeva did as the divine being asked. After the king's entourage had left, the *vidyadhara* appeared again. Giving the king more instructions, the *vidyadhara* disappeared, quick as a flash.

The king thrust his sword into the ground outside his new palace and rode away. After a while, he heard the sound of lashing waves right behind him. Vasudeva turned to look, even though the *vidyadhara* had told him expressly not to do that. That's when he realized that an ocean had indeed been following him. However, because he had looked back, the ocean instantly turned into a lake.

'I told you! I told you! I told you not to look back,' the *vidyadhara* cried, as he flew down from the orange-blue sky. 'The waters have turned into a salt lake now.

But don't worry, this lake will be with your family forever. Goddess Shakambhari be blessed – she will protect the lake herself. Look, there's her shrine! Don't you think you should thank her? I think you should.'

'Thank you, *vidyadhara*. My family will always be grateful…' Vasudeva said, but he was interrupted again by the winged being.

'It's all right. No need to thank me. Oh, how much you talk, kind king. The sun has set. I must get home. Take care, and do visit the goddess!' The *vidyadhara* vanished again, and Vasudeva got off his horse to taste the salty waters of his new lake.

To show his gratitude to the goddess, the king stayed overnight at the temple. The next morning, as the sun's rays made the shallow waters of his salt lake glisten,

he was reminded of the radiant form of the goddess. 'Shakambhari *jheel!*' he announced, pleased with his name for the waterbody.

'Ready to go home, my friend?' he asked his horse as he mounted. The animal neighed and began galloping at full speed. Vasudeva laughed and said, 'I'll take that as a "yes"!'

Connecting the Dots...

Vasudeva's kingdom was called Jangladesa. It later came to be known as Sapaadalaksha – this name refers to the 1,25,000 villages that were part of the region at that time. As per modern-day boundaries, large portions of Rajasthan, Haryana, the Shivalik Hills and beyond were part of this territory. Shakambhari jheel *(which means 'lake') is situated in the Thar Desert in Rajasthan. Its name seems to have been shortened over time, for it is known today as the Sambhar Lake. A little distance away is a temple dedicated to the goddess Shakambhari – the one that the king is believed to have visited.*

The Dynasty of the Goddess

Vasudeva was one of the founder kings of the dynasty known as the Chahamanas of Shakambhari. The Chahamana kings enjoyed a much more powerful position than their neighbouring kingdoms, thanks to their salt lake. The salt panned from this lake was traded, adding more prosperity to the Chahamana Empire. Over the years, the Chahamana kings came to be known as the Chauhans. The legendary king Prithviraj Chauhan also belonged to this dynasty. There are various versions of the legend of how King Vasudeva came to receive the salt lake as a gift. This version is taken from an English translation of a Sanskrit epic poem titled *Prithviraja Vijaya*.

The Desert Basin

The Sambhar Lake is the largest inland saltwater lake in India. Situated in the Thar Desert, it has the Aravalli Mountains lying to the west and north-west. While the waters from the rivers Mendha and Rupangarh and other smaller streams flow into it, the lake also receives water from rainfall. The lake is categorized as a 'playa'. This means that it is a desert basin where a seasonal lake forms only when it is fed by the waters from all of these sources. At other times, the lake's waters dry up because the Sambhar Lake has a shallow, endorheic basin. In an endorheic lake, the water cannot flow out of it and into another waterbody such as a sea or an ocean. The water levels of such a lake are usually lower than the level of the land around it. As a result, evaporation takes place and some shallow water with its soluble salts are left behind on the lakebed. This concentrated water, with extremely high salt levels, is called brine.

A small portion of the Sambhar Lake is a brine pool. It is separated from the main lake by a mini dam that was built to let salty water flow into the pool. Salt pans have been created in this brine pool to farm and collect salt. The brine in the Sambhar Lake appears in various colours: yellow, green, brown, pink and even red! The colour depends on the salt level of the brine and the type of algae that is present in it.

With more and more dams being built over the rivers that flow into the Sambhar Lake, its water levels have been decreasing. The rainfall too has been scanty in the region. These conditions, as well as the hot desert climate, cause the waters to evaporate and leave behind salt deposits, which are then mined and traded. Earlier, salt farming was strictly done once the lake's waters had gone down naturally. These days, however, the lake has to deal with the problem of artificial mining.

For a Pinch of Salt

Salt is a basic necessity, but it is also a thriving business. Tonnes and tonnes of salt are produced from the waters of the Sambhar Lake. Some traders have dug borewells (deep artificial wells) in the surrounding areas and installed pump and pipe sets to draw out water from deep inside the earth, and illegally mine the salt. Such misuse has upset the lake's ecosystem and affected the water levels. It has also become a huge threat to the birds that make the Sambhar Lake their home, especially the greater flamingos. If only greed could be kept miles away from the lake that had been gifted to a king who was the salt of the earth!

Vasudeva respected the saltwater lake that had magically appeared in his kingdom. But did you know that there was another king whose unmindful deed once upset a gentle river?

19

The River Daughter

Narmada

Ravana sat quietly on the banks of the Narmada. The gurgling sound of the river, the feel of its cool waters, and the secluded surroundings filled him with a deep sense of calm.

Closing his eyes, he began chanting, *'Om Namah Shivaya... Om Namah Shivaya...'*

While Ravana was lost in prayer, the river began to thin out. Then, unexpectedly, the Narmada flowed down with such force that Ravana was pushed off his seat on the banks.

Somehow, he managed to move out of the way of the rapids. Shocked and bewildered, he muttered to himself, 'Something's wrong! Why is the Narmada behaving so erratically?'

The story goes back to a time when Shiva had chosen a quiet spot in lush surroundings to sit down and meditate. Inhaling the air, which smelled of mist and the medicinal plants that grew in the area, he closed his eyes and began to focus on the rhythm of his breath.

Time flew by and seasons changed. One day, the bright sun made the pleasant weather disappear. Little droplets of sweat covered Shiva's body, but his meditation only deepened. As the heat became more extreme, so did his concentration. The sweat from his body began to trickle down onto the ground.

Shiva perspired for a long, long time. Soon, tiny, misshapen water pools began forming all around him. He continued to perspire, and the small pools merged into one another. After some time, the bigger pools slowly began flowing into a large tank-like hollow nearby.

Several days later, the god was still perspiring. Then, slowly, a gentle divine being emerged from the brimming tank. Realizing that the tank might overflow any minute, she called out, 'Father!'

Shiva did not respond. So intense was his meditation that nothing in the universe could draw him out of it.

'Father!' she tried again, a little louder this time.

Shiva felt an unusual calmness take over. He opened his eyes and realized that he was drenched in sweat. 'Strange! I feel at peace after this meditation despite the streams of perspiration,' he said to himself.

Suddenly, he noticed the young lady.

'I'm your river daughter,' she said to him.

Shiva smiled at her. 'Daughter, you shall be one of the holiest rivers in this country. For your soft and kind nature, I name you Narmada. Whoever watches you flow by, or sits on your banks quietly, will find inner peace,' he said, blessing her.

Bowing to Shiva, Narmada went back into the tank from which she had appeared. Snaking gracefully out of it, she began flowing like a river. Travelling through the landscape, over smooth pebbles and sharp rocks, she gave life to places along her course.

Mahishmati was one such place. Little did Narmada know then that her banks in Mahishmati would become the site of a battle between two superwarriors one day, thus ruining Shiva's well-meaning blessing.

The battle occurred years later, when the kingdom of Mahishmati was ruled by an able king called Kartavirya Arjuna. He was believed to be the human incarnation of Vishnu's spinning disc, the *sudarshan chakra*. Dattatreya, the god who was the single, composite avatar of the three gods – Brahma, Vishnu and Shiva – had given Kartavirya the boon of having a thousand arms and hands! Since the Sanskrit word *sahasra* means 'thousand', Kartavirya came to be known as Sahasrarjuna. His arms opened out like a disc, making him resemble his original form.

One day, Sahasrarjuna's queens expressed a collective wish. 'We want you to control the waters of the Narmada. We want to bathe and play in the river without worrying about drifting away.'

'Control Narmada's flow? How can I do that?' Sahasrarjuna asked, amused.

'Well, you have a thousand arms,' one of his queens said, shrugging.

Giving in, Sahasrarjuna went with his queens to the river.

Around the same time, Ravana, the ten-headed king of Lanka, was travelling above the Narmada in his flying chariot, the Pushpaka Vimana. He was looking for a tranquil place to offer his daily prayers to Shiva, his favourite god. Seeing the waters of the Narmada glistening like diamonds under the sun, Ravana thought, *the banks are perfect for my prayers.*

Descending from the Pushpaka Vimana, he settled on the banks. He picked up an oval stone from the riverbank, fixed it in the sand, decorated it with flowers, and lit a few mud lamps around it. For Ravana, the oval stone was a symbol of Shiva. Then, he began his prayers, and the air reverberated with his chants.

Meanwhile, the atmosphere upstream was filled with the animated laughter of Sahasrarjuna's queens. The thousand-armed king had stopped the river from flowing ahead so that the queens could play to their hearts' content in the surging water.

Slowly, the river began thinning downstream, where Ravana sat and prayed, oblivious to this sudden change.

Although Narmada wasn't comfortable with Sahasrarjuna's actions, she stayed put. He was a good king, and he didn't mean the river any harm. But beyond a point, Narmada couldn't contain herself. She had to flow freely. Unable to control her flow any longer, she began slipping away from both sides of Sahasrarjuna's outstretched arms.

Pushed forward by the force of all the collected water, Narmada dived downstream wildly. She noticed Ravana and the Shiva *linga* (the oval stone symbolizing the god) in her path, but it was too late. She crashed into them and washed away the flowers and the lamps.

When a confused Ravana reached upstream to investigate, he saw Sahasrarjuna still trying to stop the flow of Narmada and the waters escaping out from the sides.

'Fool!' Ravana yelled. 'Why would you control a river's waters? Just to prove your strength? Do you know what has happened downstream?'

Sahasrarjuna realized his mistake. He gently lowered his thousand arms and let the river flow along her course. 'We didn't know you were down there,' he said, as his queens swam out of the river hurriedly.

'You have ruined my prayers and disrespected my Shiva,' Ravana raged. 'Just because you have a thousand arms, do you think you can get away with anything?'

Before Sahasrarjuna could reply, Ravana challenged him, 'If you are a true warrior, show *me* your strength.'

'I said we didn't know you were down there. But if you still wish to fight, I'm ready!' Sahasrarjuna retorted.

As Narmada watched helplessly, the two warriors got into a long, difficult battle. They seemed equally matched until Sahasrarjuna twirled Ravana with some of his arms, pinned him down and tied his hands together

with his silk sash. He then noticed a few mud lamps, some ghee and wicks lying on the riverbank. So, with his other arms, Sahasrarjuna picked eleven mud lamps out of the sand, poured ghee and placed wicks in each one and lit them up. He then placed one mud lamp on each of Ravana's ten foreheads and one over his tied palms.

As Sahasrajauna stepped away, the setting sun formed a red-orange aura behind him. Even in his defeated state, Ravana understood who Sahasrarjuna truly was: 'Vishnu's *sudarshan chakra*!'

Ravana then noticed Narmada from the corner of his eyes. She seemed sad to have witnessed this pointless fight. For the sake of Shiva and his river daughter, he surely could have tried to resolve the matter peacefully, he rued.

Connecting the Dots...

Quite a few rivers originate from the Satpura, Vindhya, and Maikal mountain ranges, which are situated in central India. Cradled by these three ranges, the picturesque region of Amarkantak was where Shiva sat in deep meditation. For the important role it plays in geomythology, Amarkantak is popularly called Teertharaj, which means the 'king of pilgrimages'. The River Narmada, which originates in the Maikal range in Amarkantak, snakes through parts of present-day Madhya Pradesh, Maharashtra and Gujarat.

Maheshwar, a town in Madhya Pradesh, along which the Narmada flows, is believed to be the site of the ancient kingdom of Mahishmati. Even today, in the Sahasrarjuna Temple in Maheshwar, 11 lamps are lit to celebrate the thousand-armed king's victory over the ten-headed Ravana.

However, in a strange mythological twist, Sahasrarjuna (an incarnation of Vishnu's sudarshan chakra, *as mentioned in the story) was later defeated by Parashurama (an avatar of Vishnu), for having killed the warrior-sage's father, Sage Jamdagni.*

Narmada Parikrama

Many people consider Narmada to be a sacred river, a status that Shiva had bestowed upon his river daughter. Devotees worship the river by walking clockwise around its full length but without crossing it.

They begin their journey from Mithi Talai in Bharuch, Gujarat, where the river's mouth meets the Arabian Sea. From here, they walk up to the river's source in Amarkantak, Madhya Pradesh. Then, going around to the other side of the river, they walk back all the way to Bharuch. Some begin the journey from the source in Amarkantak, go around the mouth in Mithi Talai and then head back to Amarkantak.

This sacred tour is known as Narmada Parikrama – in Sanskrit, *parikrama* means 'to walk or go around something in a full circle'. Can you guess how long this round trip takes? Three years, three months and thirteen days!

The Meander of a Pleasing River

The Narmada was known as Nerbudda (also spelt Narbada) when India was under British rule. Narmada Kund, a water tank in the Amarkantak plateau of Madhya Pradesh, is the source of the river. With a length of 1,312 kilometres, Narmada is the fifth-largest river in India.

Over millions of years, the collision of the Indian plate with the Eurasian plate and other tectonic movements have constantly changed the physical features of the river. Shiva may have named the waterbody Narmada after her gentle nature, but it sure is a tough river! It flows over both flat and rocky terrain. In some places, its waters flow as smooth channels, and elsewhere as a frothy stream. In other places, it tumbles down as a waterfall from a gorge.

The most famous of the Narmada's falls is Dhuandhar, which cascades from the Bhedaghat Gorge in Jabalpur, Madhya Pradesh. Bhedaghat is known for its looming, whitish marble rocks. A boat ride on the Narmada's waters that flow below these towering rocks makes for a most thrilling geotourism experience! Geotourism, short for geological tourism, is a term used to describe the tour of geographical wonders.

Over the years, the river's flow has been artificially stopped and altered as well. No, Sahasrarjuna isn't standing in its path today! But the many dams built over it have halted its waters, just as he had tried to do. In this case too, Narmada's haphazard flow has been causing destruction – washing away crops, killing fish and making people lose their homes and livelihoods.

The Raja and the Hominin

Apart from Sahasrarjuna and Ravana, another royal being is also associated with the Narmada – a dinosaur species called Rajasaurus ('lizard king')! Fossils found in the region suggest that millions of years ago, dinosaurs walked along the river's banks. Who knows, maybe they went around and did a *parikrama* too? The remains of flying dinosaurs with wings as wide as 30 feet have also been discovered by archaeologists in the Narmada Valley in Madhya Pradesh. They would have enjoyed the aerial view of the river as well, just as Ravana did from his Pushpaka Vimana!

But one of the most important finds has been the fossilized skullcap of an individual from the hominin group. Hominins are a sub-group of the primate family, and their only existing descendants today are the *Homo sapiens* or the modern human beings.

Excavated in 1982, this skull fragment is the first-ever hominin fossil to have been recovered from India. Since the fossil was found near the Hathnora village in the Narmada Valley, this hominin has been nicknamed the 'Narmada Human'. Some experts say the Narmada Human may have lived here anywhere between five to six lakh years ago! How old could the river be then?

An Epic Journey

The epics Mahabharata and the Ramayana, which narrate the stories of two complex royal families, set the journeys undertaken by their lead characters in real locations. Thus, geographical features such as the Panchchuli Peaks, Satopanth Lake and the Swargarohini Glacier, situated in the Himalayas, have actually got their names from specific episodes in the Mahabharata!

The Ramayana too maps the trail followed by its protagonists – the princes Rama and Lakshmana. Theirs was no ordinary journey. For, as they travelled on, they witnessed earth-shattering battles, had an ingenious bridge built, and even caused drastic changes to a distant landscape!

20

Of Beaten Brothers and Broken Boulders

Hampi

Sugreeva stood over a high rock and scanned his kingdom grimly. There were huge monoliths all around, with patches of green vegetation carpeting the ground.

'Never thought I'd live to see the day I'd stand against my own brother!' he sighed.

Looking at the huge rocks made him sadder. After all, it was one such boulder that had changed his life.

Not so long ago, the *vanara* Sugreeva and his brother, Vali, had been inseparable. The *vanaras* were a group of forest dwellers, whose kingdom was called Kishkindha, and Vali was their king.

No one dared to challenge Vali, for he was one of the most powerful warriors of his time. But one day, a demon named Mayavi did exactly that. It was only during the fight that Mayavi realized that he had made a huge mistake. He figured out that the only way to survive Vali's wrath was to run. And so, he camouflaged himself among the monoliths that dotted Kishkindha and slunk into a cave. But Vali and Sugreeva followed him there.

'Whatever happens, do not come in,' Vali whispered to Sugreeva.

'*B-but*, brother…' the latter protested.

'This is *my* fight, Sugreeva. Wait for me here, till I come back.' And Vali disappeared into the cave.

Hearing Mayavi's cries for help, Sugreeva shook his head. 'Silly of him to have challenged Vali in the first place. He's paying for his overconfidence!'

The fight went on and on. Days later, Sugreeva, who was waiting outside the cave, heard Vali cry out sharply in pain.

Sugreeva's heart sank. He wanted to go in, but he remembered what he had promised his brother. So, he waited and waited. There was no sound thereafter.

Months later, he caught a glimpse of the demon at the far end of the cave.

'Mayavi!' Sugreeva exclaimed. 'But where is Vali? He should have followed Mayavi. Why can't I see or hear him?' Every now and then, such questions clouded his mind. But he managed to calm himself down and continued to wait.

An entire year passed, yet Sugreeva didn't budge from the place. One evening, a stream of blood flowed out of the cave. Fear gripped Sugreeva. 'Has Mayavi killed Vali? No, it can't be!'

Then, another thought occurred to him. 'If Vali is indeed dead, Mayavi will emerge from the cave any moment now, and cause mayhem in Kishkindha. I can't let that happen. I must trap Mayavi in this cave forever!' And Sugreeva shut the cave's entrance with a huge boulder.

Gloom descended upon Kishkindha, but the *vanaras* had to elect a new king.

'Who better than Sugreeva? He has saved us from Mayavi,' one of the courtiers suggested.

So, Sugreeva was crowned the king of Kishkindha. But fate had other plans. Days later, the boulder blocking the entrance of the cave – the one that Sugreeva had put in place – was shattered into a million pieces by a strong fist. Out came Vali, having successfully defeated Mayavi!

When he returned to the palace and saw Sugreeva on the throne, Vali went mad with rage. 'My *own* brother, the one I've loved so dearly, has turned against me!' he yelled, storming into the royal court.

Sugreeva ran to hug him. 'Brother, you're alive!'

'Don't pretend now! You wanted me dead, so you shut the cave and crowned yourself king!'

'*N-no*, that's not true. Please, let me explain!' Sugreeva begged, falling at Vali's feet.

Vali walked off and sat on the throne. 'A traitor like you has no place here. If I see you anywhere, *anywhere*...' he said, glaring at Sugreeva.

The *vanaras* in the court looked at each other. *Sugreeva wouldn't lie*, they thought. *Or would he?*

Unable to bear the piercing glances everyone shot at him, Sugreeva left the palace. He knew Vali would kill him if he saw him again, so he went into hiding. Some *vanaras* stayed loyal to Sugreeva and followed him – they felt that Vali's decision to banish him had been unfair.

Around this time, Rama and Lakshmana, the princes of Ayodhya, were passing through Kishkindha. They were on the trail of Ravana, the king of Lanka, who had kidnapped Rama's wife, Sita. In Kishkindha, they met Sugreeva through Hanuman, the mighty *vanara* who was the son of Vayu (the god of wind). Hanuman, a supporter of Sugreeva and a loyal friend to Rama, had introduced them in the hope that they would help each other.

'The *vanaras* are with you in your fight against Ravana. We will help you reach Lanka,' Sugreeva promised.

'And we are with you in your fight against your brother,' Lakshmana said.

'Yes, I will help you win back the throne from Vali,' Rama said.

'But how? My brother is extremely strong. And he has a boon – anyone who fights him loses half their strength and powers to him!' Sugreeva said.

'If *your* brother is the greatest warrior you know, let me tell you that *my* brother is the greatest of the great! No boon can stop his victory! He'll surely find a way to beat Vali,' Lakshmana said confidently.

The group decided that Sugreeva would challenge Vali to a duel. It was on the morning of this fight that

Sugreeva stood on a rock, surveying the kingdom. The time to win it back had come.

A fierce battle ensued between the *vanara* brothers. Rama, who was hiding behind a tree some distance away, was ready to shoot an arrow at Vali. But this was a battle like none that he had seen before.

Vali and Sugreeva uprooted the huge monoliths that Kishkindha was famous for and hurled them at each other. The mountain-like stones came crashing down, falling into heaps of large boulders. The other *vanaras*

cowered in fear. The sound was deafening, and the earth shook violently.

Dodging a giant rock hurled at him in the middle of the fight, Sugreeva rushed towards Rama. 'I thought you were helping me? His boon is making me lose my powers,' he said nervously.

'I *am* trying to help, Sugreeva. But you and Vali look so alike. What if I shoot you by mistake?' Rama replied. He was right. Vali and Sugreeva looked so similar that even some of the *vanaras* found it difficult to tell them apart.

That's when Hanuman had an idea. He produced a garland from somewhere and put it around Sugreeva's neck. 'This should help,' he told Rama.

Another rock came crashing down near Sugreeva and the others.

'Oh, aren't you bored of throwing these rocks around? How about a fist fight?' Vali called out to Sugreeva.

The brothers then began wrestling. Sugreeva, even though he'd lost half his powers to Vali, continued to put up a good fight. Then, at the right moment, Rama released an arrow – a straight shot, it pierced Vali's heart.

The prince rushed to the dying *vanara*.

'Why?' Vali managed to ask Rama, seeing that the famous prince of Ayodhya had chosen to take his brother's side. He felt very let down by Sugreeva as well as Rama.

'You didn't give Sugreeva a chance to explain himself. Your anger blinded you to the truth. It turned a beloved brother into an arch-enemy. Your anger made the *vanaras* feel that Sugreeva was a better choice for a king. And *that* is what led to your downfall, Vali,' Rama said.

Tears trickled down Vali's hairy face. He hugged Sugreeva one last time and murmured, 'Brother!'

That evening, Sugreeva surveyed Kishkindha once again. The monoliths were gone, just like his brother. All that remained were fragmented boulders.

Connecting the Dots...

The ancient kingdom of the vanaras, *Kishkindha, is said to have been located where Hampi in Karnataka stands today. People believe that the huge rocks found all over Hampi tell the tale of the broken relationship between the* vanara *brothers Vali and Sugreeva.*

Hampi is located over the Dharwar Craton. The word craton comes from the Greek word kratos, *which means 'strength'. In the context of geography it signifies the strength of an unchanging block of land. In the case of Hampi, it seems to signify the strength of both – the region's boulders and the* vanara *brothers.*

A Balancing Act

A craton is a vast block of the earth's crust (the outermost layer), which has not changed very much over billions of years. The Indian Shield, the part of the Indian peninsula which looks like an inverted triangle, includes five stable cratons. One of these is the Dharwar Craton, which is also known as the Karnataka Craton.

The Dharwar Craton is divided into the Western Dharwar Craton and the Eastern Dharwar Craton, based on the differences in how the cratons were formed, as well as the rock systems found there. Hampi is part of the Eastern Dharwar Craton. The landscape of Hampi is distinctive, for it has numerous granite boulders strewn around in piles. Some of these rock stacks are as tall as actual hills!

So, who piled up the boulders? According to geologists, Hampi's unique landscape was formed due to the weathering of the gigantic monoliths that existed here several million years ago. Weathering is erosion caused by natural or seasonal factors such as harsh sunlight, strong winds and heavy rainfall.

Over the years, the monoliths developed cracks and fell apart – these broken blocks came crashing down and sat one on top of another as boulders. Erosion also gave these boulders smooth surfaces and their oval and circular shapes. In many places, groups of boulders are naturally stacked over one another in such a precarious way that they have formed balancing rocks.

An Architectural Wonder

Hampi is home to historic palaces and temples built by Emperor Krishna Deva Raya of the Vijayanagara Empire, who ruled over the region from 1509 to 1529 CE. Much of Vijayanagara's architecture was fashioned from the grey and pinkish-brown granite rocks found in the region. However, the kingdom was designed in such a way that several of the boulder heaps were kept intact, and the structures were built *around* them – the empire surely knew how to respect the wonders of geography! Today, the boulders of Hampi, along with the Vijayanagara monuments, are a UNESCO World Heritage Site.

Vali and Sugreeva willingly broke down the monoliths of their kingdom in a battle, thus changing Kishkindha's landscape. But did you know that there was a time when Rama had no choice but to dry up a lush land?

21

An Unfortunate Target

Thar

'You can't possibly dry up an entire ocean!' Varuna said exasperatedly.

'I can. Watch me,' said Rama, pulling back the divine arrow and bowstring as he took aim.

'Stop! Stop!' Varuna pleaded. 'All right, let me think!'

Rama nodded and waited. Lakshmana, Hanuman and the *vanaras* watched Varuna as he paced up and down on the ocean, creating choppy waves.

Suddenly, he stopped. Looking wide-eyed at Rama, Varuna said, 'I think I've found a solution!'

After winning back the throne of Kishkindha from Vali, Sugreeva had entrusted Hanuman with the task of helping Rama and Lakshmana find Sita. When Hanuman visited Ravana's kingdom in Lanka, he found out where Sita was being held captive. He offered to rescue her immediately, but she wanted Rama to come to Lanka himself and vanquish Ravana. Only then would she go home.

The mighty *vanara* promptly returned to Kishkindha and relayed all this to the princes of Ayodhya.

Rama, Lakshmana and the entire *vanara* army began marching towards Lanka. But on the way, they faced a new challenge.

'There is an entire ocean between our land and Lanka,' Lakshmana said, standing at the edge of the land, wringing his hands.

'How did *you* go?' Nala, the son of the divine architect, Vishwakarma, asked Hanuman.

'I flew over it, Nala,' Hanuman said matter-of-factly. Being the son of Vayu, the wind god, Hanuman had many superpowers, and one of them was being able to fly!

'Right, what do *we* do now?' wondered Nala.

Rama, who was standing beside Lakshmana, called out: 'O Varuna, god of the oceans and seas, I request you to grant us a path through these waters. We need to travel to Lanka to rescue Sita.'

There was no response. The soft waves continued to flow over and then pull away from Rama's feet.

'Can you hear me, Varuna?' said Rama, a little louder this time.

Again, there was no response.

'Varuna, I know you can hear me…' Rama said, taking a deep breath.

Still, there was no response.

'All right, don't say I didn't warn you…' said a visibly annoyed Rama, as he nocked a deadly divine arrow.

'There's nothing I can do now, Varuna. This arrow cannot be called back. If it leaves my bow, the ocean will turn dry,' Rama said.

'No, please!' said an anxious Varuna, appearing at last. 'Don't shoot. I didn't answer because I honestly cannot help you. If I part the ocean, it will cause mayhem – even you know that, Prince Rama.'

'It's too late now. You could have just told me this before. This is a divine arrow, and I cannot put it back in,' Rama sighed.

Varuna paced about and then finally came up with a solution. 'You can build a bridge over the ocean. You have Vishwakarma's son Nala with you.'

'Sure, I can do it,' Nala chimed in. 'But wait – the arrow!'

'Oh right.' Varuna thought about it for a few seconds and said, 'Can you divert the arrow? There's a place to the north-west of this ocean. If you could aim that way…'

'And *why* would I do that?' Rama asked.

'There's a gang of robbers hiding in a forest near the banks of a river. Your divine arrow will frighten them and rescue the region's inhabitants,' Varuna suggested.

'Hmm…sounds fair,' Rama said, and turned in the opposite direction. Touching the bow and the arrow to his forehead, he took aim and let the arrow fly.

So perfect was his aim that the divine weapon struck the exact spot where the robbers were.

Just as Varuna had said, the loud boom of the arrow tearing through the sky and landing near them scared the robbers witless. They ran for their lives, not looking back even once. The people of that land, who saw this miracle, rejoiced.

But Rama's arrow also had an unexpected effect. As it was a weapon initially drawn to dry up an ocean, it shook the earth and changed the course of the river flowing nearby. In a flash, the waters went underground. The lush forest around it disappeared, and the wet earth turned into sand.

The green landscape was now a hot desert.

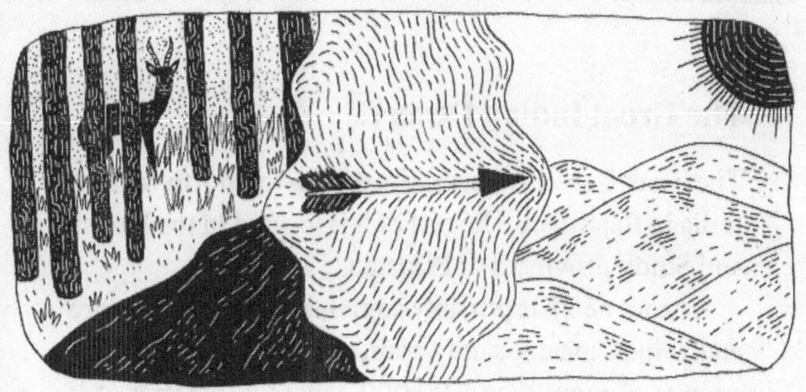

Connecting the Dots...

People believe that Ravana's kingdom was situated where present-day Sri Lanka is. The ocean, from which Varuna emerged, is believed to be the Indian Ocean. Even today, this vast waterbody separates India and Sri Lanka. The tropical forest where the robbers were hiding, which turned dry on being struck by Rama's arrow, is known today as the Thar Desert.

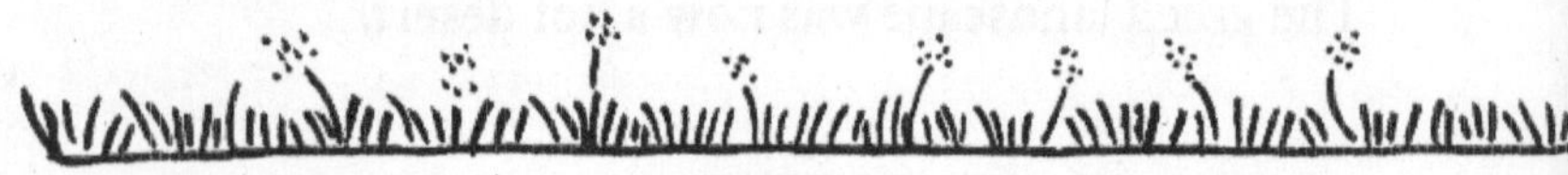

The Great Indian Desert

The Thar Desert is partly situated in the north-west of India in Rajasthan. The rest of it is located in the Punjab and Sindh provinces of Pakistan.

The name Thar possibly comes from the Hindi word *thal*, which means 'sandy plain' or 'dry land'. Covering an area of more than 2,00,000 square kilometres, it is the largest desert in the country. That explains why it is also known as the Great Indian Desert!

Researchers have found that around a million years ago, the region was home to a verdant forest. It was irrigated by many rivers and received good rainfall as well. But the movement of tectonic plates caused the course of the rivers which flowed through this region to change. And soon, wide rivers became thin streams. Archaeological finds from the region suggest that the *Homo erectus* (the ancestor of modern humans) lived and hunted on this land – stone tools recovered from the area are proof of such a civilization. Archaeologists have also found evidence that thousands of years ago, jamun trees thrived here.

However, rainfall began to decline over time, and the once-fertile land became dry. The rivers flowed further away or got buried deep below the earth. Strong winds brought in silt and sand. As sand grains were continuously deposited over several years, they formed sand dunes. The most fascinating thing about these dunes is that they keep moving and shifting. Due to the westerly winds that blow over the Thar, the desert looks different every day!

Although the landscape and the climate changed around them, humans learnt to adapt to the parched terrain, and today, the Thar is said to be the world's most populated desert.

Around 300 kilometres away, in the Mokalawas village of Jodhpur district, stands Arna Jharna – the Thar Desert Museum, which preserves the folk culture of Rajasthan's communities. It houses photographs, audiovisual recordings, species of desert flora, and an array of objects, especially musical instruments. One of these, the *ravanahatta*, is a stringed instrument named after the ten-headed king, Ravana!

The Unseen River

The stream that flowed through the forest which disappeared is said to have been the sacred Saraswati. Even though some water channels have been traced along the Thar Desert, a few researchers believe that there is not enough proof to establish the Saraswati's existence.

However, some archaeologists who have been studying the region suggest that the Saraswati was not a mythical river, and that it actually existed. Others say that the Saraswati is the same as the Ghaggar-Hakra River, which originates from the Shivalik Hills in Himachal Pradesh and flows through Punjab and Haryana today, before making its way to the Thar. A seasonal river, the Ghaggar-Hakra comes alive only during the monsoon.

Rama's diverted arrow ended up transforming a once-lush land into the barren expanse of the Thar. But did you know that there was yet another piece of land that Rama was asked to destroy?

22

The Bow at the Edge of a Beach

Dhanushkodi

The *vanara* army looked distraught. 'If every stone we throw into the ocean sinks, it will take years to construct a bridge that is visible above the water. How are we *ever* going to finish this task?' one of the *vanaras* asked Nala, the architect of the bridge. Nala knelt on the shore and looked at the heap of stones that the army had collected.

Hanuman, who had been watching all this from a distance, began singing loudly:

'The architect's plan is all clear,
But the stones are sinking – oh dear!
So, how do we make the stones adhere?
Don't you worry, Hanuman is here!'

Nala, who had the responsibility of building a bridge over the ocean to reach Lanka, began making a plan.

With the edge of a stick that he had found nearby, he drew a diagram in the moist sand.

'Brilliant!' he exclaimed, appreciating his own plan, although no one around understood any of it.

Nala then put the entire *vanara* army to work. 'We have no time to waste and no time to rest. Bring the biggest, largest, hugest stones and boulders you can find to this spot,' he told them. The *vanara*s leapt away in different directions to find suitable boulders. Soon, they had collected enough in all shapes and sizes.

'Now start throwing the stones you collected into the water. The idea is to build a floating bridge. Got it?' he said.

The *vanara*s nodded and quickly formed a queue. Each of them held a large stone. The plan was to throw the stones one after the other. The first *vanara* in the queue threw the stone he was holding into the ocean.

Splash!

The stone sank immediately.

The *vanara* who was right behind him carrying another huge stone burst out laughing. 'You shouldn't throw it with such force. Watch me,' he said, and threw his stone in carefully.

Splish! This stone floated for a second longer than the earlier one, but it sank too. It was now the turn of the *vanara* behind them to laugh at the failed attempts of his friends.

This went on for a while. One by one, the *vanaras* threw stones into the water, but none managed to stay afloat. Frustrated, they turned to Nala for help.

It was while Nala was examining the boulders to understand why they were sinking that Hanuman had begun singing to annoy him. Nala rolled his eyes.

'All we have to do is make them light,' Hanuman said, lifting one of them.

'You can't change the very nature of the stone, Hanuman,' Rama said, amused by the exchange.

'I can!'

Hanuman picked up a small chalk-like rock and wrote a single word on the large boulder – *Rama.*

Lakshmana laughed as the *vanara* army looked at each other, confused.

Nala was sceptical too, but before he could say anything, Hanuman threw the boulder into the water. 'It feels quite light now,' he said.

To everyone's surprise, the huge boulder began to float. Nala waited to see if it would sink, but it just gently bobbed up and down on the waves.

'There, Nala! We can build the Rama Setu now!' Hanuman quipped.

'Hurrah!' the army shouted as Nala smiled and nodded at Hanuman.

He then directed some of the *vanaras* to help Hanuman. They sat around the collected pile of boulders and began writing the prince's name on each one.

Meanwhile, the other *vanaras* went about laying the unique floating bridge.

'The bridge is ready,' Nala told Rama after five days.

As the princes and the *vanaras* crossed the bridge, they realized that even though the stones were floating, they were strong enough to carry the weight of the entire army!

On reaching Lanka, a terrible war took place between Rama's army and Ravana's forces, which consisted of some formidable warriors, like his son Meghanada, and his giant brother, Kumbhakarna.

One of Ravana's other brothers though, the righteous Vibhishana, chose to ally with Rama.

The battle went on for days. Finally, Ravana himself entered the battlefield to fight Rama. The prince didn't realize that Ravana's ten heads were a boon. Every time Rama beheaded Ravana, another head emerged, giving him a new lease of life.

With blessings from Goddess Durga, Rama then shot a divine arrow straight at Ravana's navel – this was the only way to take off all his heads at once, and thus end his life. The ten-headed king of Lanka was finally defeated, and Sita was reunited with Rama.

Vibhishana was crowned the new king of Lanka. As Rama and his army got ready to return to their land through the floating bridge that they had constructed, Vibhishana made a request. 'Please break this bridge down once you reach the other end, Prince Rama.'

'But why?' Rama asked. 'It will help your people and ours travel easily.'

'True, but it can also be misused by invaders!' said Vibhishana.

Understanding his concern, Rama promised to fulfil his request. And so, upon returning from Lanka, Rama shot a number of arrows to break the bridge. Several stones broke apart and sank, while only a few remained afloat.

Then, Rama struck his bow with all his might at the edge of the land, which was still connected to a large part of the bridge. *Boom!*

Immediately, the remnants of the bridge sank into the water. All that remained visible over the ocean were the floating fragments of boulders, a reminder that a bridge once existed between these two lands.

Connecting the Dots...

A bridge, which is visible between the Gulf of Mannar (on the Indian Ocean side) and the Palk Bay (on the Bay of Bengal side), is believed to be the one built by the vanara *army. Connecting the Dhanushkodi Beach on Rameswaram Island in Tamil Nadu to Mannar Island in Sri Lanka, this strip of land is called Rama Setu (Rama's Bridge). As Nala was the architect, it is also known as Nala Setu (Nala's Bridge). In Sanskrit,* setu *means 'bridge'.*

The place where Rama struck his bow, to separate the bridge from the mainland, came to be known as Dhanushkodi – in Tamil, the name means 'corner or edge where the bow was struck', as dhanush *means 'bow', and* kodi *means 'corner' or 'edge'. Dhanushkodi, which is a beach, lies at the south-eastern tip of Rameswaram Island (also known as Pamban Island).*

The Sacred Step

There is a well-known summit in Sri Lanka which bears a large footprint in stone. This footprint is dear to people of different communities in both countries, and each group has its own story about it.

Hindus believe that it belongs to Shiva. Buddhists say the Buddha's foot impression was engraved on the peak when he took a long stride from there and crossed over to Thailand. Christians believe that Saint Thomas, who spread the teachings of Christianity through the region, left his footprint there.

Muslims believe that this was the peak where Adam first set foot on earth. Adam and Eve, believed to be the first human couple by Abrahamic religions, initially lived in the heavenly Garden of Eden. However, when they disobeyed the Supreme Being and ate the fruit of a forbidden tree, they were sent to live in the world of mortals as punishment, and as Adam descended to earth, his large footprint came to be etched there. It is also said that Adam walked from the peak to the mainland of India using the bridge that connected the two lands. This is why the sacred summit in Sri Lanka is known as Adam's Peak, and the floating pathway between the two countries is also called Adam's Bridge.

Bound by a Bridge

Satellite images show a ridge-like formation, partially above the water and partially underwater, running between the Indian peninsula and the island of Sri Lanka. It is said that a fully visible bridge connected India and Sri Lanka once, but it was destroyed by a cyclone in 1480 CE.

There are many theories about how the Rama Setu came to be. To begin with, some believe that it was made by humans, while others say it is a geological formation.

Even among those who feel that it is a natural wonder, different views on how the bridge must have actually been formed exist. One theory goes back to the time when Pangaea broke apart, eventually leading to the formation of the Indian subcontinent. At that time, Sri Lanka was a part of this large mass of land. Over time, as the plates continued to move, the part which forms present-day Sri Lanka separated from the mainland, the Indian subcontinent. When this separation took place, a trail of smaller parts of land was left behind, forming a fragmented ridge between the two countries.

Some experts say that the ridge is made of limestone, and consists of a submerged, ribbon-like sandbank. Since sand is deposited by ocean currents and winds over a period of time, researchers say that newer sediments are constantly changing the shape of the ridge. Another view is that the coral reefs across this stretch have trapped sand, creating the partly visible bridge. According to yet another perspective, the many shifts in the land positions have caused the water levels to change, and this is why the bridge is sometimes visible and invisible at other times. The theories are many, and will go on being formulated until more discoveries are made.

Of Grit and a Ghost Town

More than a century ago, Dhanushkodi Beach was known for not just the Rama Setu, but for another bridge as well – the Pamban Railway Bridge, which connected the mainland with Rameswaram Island and this beach town. In 1964, India was hit by a severe cyclone, in which Dhanushkodi – a thriving trade hub between India and Sri Lanka then – was wiped out overnight. At the time the cyclone struck, a train was passing through the Pamban Railway Bridge. A gigantic wave rose from the sea, swallowing the Pamban–Dhanushkodi stretch of the bridge as well as the train full of passengers in a single sweep.

The rest of the bridge remained almost intact, and is more than 100 years old today! A modern, mechanized Pamban Railway Bridge still exists between the mainland and Rameswaram Island. This is India's first vertical-lift railway bridge – its technology is so amazing that when the bridge remains horizontal, trains pass over it. And, when it opens up vertically, smaller ships pass underneath it! Interestingly, the waters are so shallow in this region (and over Rama Setu too) that large ships have to travel around Sri Lanka, when going from one side of the sea to the other!

While a part of the railway bridge withstood the deadly cyclone, nothing survived in Dhanushkodi – except ruins, partially buried in a vast blanket of white sand. Ever since, Dhanushkodi has been called a 'ghost town' that is not fit for human inhabitation. Yet, a few fisherfolk continue to make the isolated beach their home.

From the rocky terrain of Hampi and the desert dunes of Thar to the abandoned shores of Dhanushkodi, human beings have learnt to survive in some pretty difficult terrain, don't you think?

Conflicts and Change

Change is at the core of geography, not just triggered by the wars between gods and giants, but often by objects from outer space, the constant rise and fall of water levels, shifting plates, natural disasters and the destruction of resources by humans.

In the tussle between man and the environment, it is difficult to say who will emerge victorious. Yet, there's one thing that nature teaches us – that the universe will always find a way to maintain the balance! At least, that's what the stories tell us!

23

A Meteoric Strike

Lonar

'Where's your arrogant brother?' the young boy asked.

At first, the girls didn't give him a clear answer. But one of them finally pointed towards a large mound. 'There,' she said. 'Below that hill is his den!'

Heading straight to the hill, the boy uprooted it with a single hand. 'Lonasura!' he yelled.

Lonasura was a trouble-making giant. Along with his sisters, he had come to live in a quiet hilly region. And as soon as he had settled into his new home beneath a large hill, the giant began wreaking havoc in the neighbourhood. His sisters weren't too happy with his behaviour, but they knew that chiding him would only mean inviting his wrath.

The people of the surrounding villages were now always afraid, thinking about what the giant might do next. One day, while Lonasura was terrorizing the inhabitants of a nearby settlement, an old man shouted, 'Have some shame, Lonasura! The gods are watching. If you don't stop this right away, they'll surely send a powerful warrior to put an end to your nonsense!'

The giant laughed uproariously. 'Ooooh, I'm so scared! Let's see... Whom should the gods send to fight me? Surya? Nah! Indra, then? Pah! Ah yes, Vishnu – now he's a worthy opponent, what say?'

Suddenly growing in size, the giant looked towards the sky. 'Hey Vishnu! You there? I, Lonasura, challenge you. You hear me?' he called out.

He then stomped his right foot with such force that the earth shook, and the homes around him crumbled to dust.

That night, the people of the settlement prayed to Vishnu – only he could save them from the giant now. But the skies gave no sign in response to their prayers, and the blue god made no appearance either.

A few days later, a young boy appeared out of nowhere. Clad in a simple white dhoti, he walked through all the villages in the hilly region. For anyone he met, he had only one question: 'Hello there! Have you seen Lonasura?'

The old man who had told Lonasura off earlier was intrigued. 'Why, what business do you have with him?' he asked the child.

'Oh, nothing! I'm tired of his atrocities, so I thought I'd finish him off for good,' the boy said casually.

The man laughed. 'Be careful, boy. You might just run into him.' And he went back into his house, while the boy continued his search.

Reaching the woods that surrounded a large hill, the boy shouted, 'Lonasura! Come out, you wriggling rat!'

Lonasura's sisters, who were picking fruit, sniggered when they heard the boy.

'Such a young lad calling *our* brother a rat! *Sooo* funny!' said one of them.

Hearing them cackle, the boy went straight towards the girls and asked them about their brother's whereabouts. And that is how he came to find Lonasura lazing around in his den, beneath the hill.

'Who dared to take away the roof of my home?' Lonasura roared.

'I did!' the boy replied. 'Come out, you squiggly earthworm! I've come to squash you!'

Lonasura stared at the boy for a couple of seconds. He noticed that his face shone like the sun. Then, Lonasura began chuckling uncontrollably.

'Of all the forms in the world, Vishnu, *this* is the one you picked to fight me? Seriously?' the giant asked.

Without warning, Lonasura punched him. The boy staggered, but didn't lose his balance. A fist fight began between them.

Meanwhile, a villager, who had seen the boy lift the hill with one hand, had rushed to the surrounding settlements and informed the people about what was happening. Soon, the locals gathered at a distance to watch this strange battle between the giant and the little boy. Clouds of dust engulfed the two warriors. They continued to fight for a long, long time, but the onlookers could see nothing.

Slowly, when the dust settled, they saw two forms – Lonasura was lying on the ground and the young boy was standing on his abdomen. With folded hands, the giant was pleading with the boy to forgive him and set him free.

'I'll let you go, Lonasura, but to a place from where you can never come back!'

The boy stomped his right foot on the giant's abdomen with such force that the ground beneath him gave way, and Lonasura was thrust deep into the earth, never to be seen again.

The huge crater, which was formed as the giant crashed down, filled up with a murky liquid.

The old man who had warned the giant before, and had been watching the fight from afar, cried out in joy, 'Praise the great Vishnu, the demon slayer, the *daitya sudan*!'

The others repeated after him, 'Praise the *daitya sudan*!'

They were free once again, for all their fears now lay buried in the depths of the land.

Connecting the Dots...

The crater created by the young boy (who was clearly Vishnu), as he thrust the giant into the earth, lies in the Buldhana district in Maharashtra.

It is a local belief that Lonasura still lives at the bottom of the hollow into which he was hurled.

The lake that was formed when the crater filled with water and the town near it are both known as Lonar – after the giant Lonasura of course!

Etched in Stone

A temple dedicated to Daitya Sudan (Vishnu's avatar as the young boy) is located near the crater lake in Lonar. The temple's main idol depicts Daitya Sudan standing over Lonasura's abdomen as the giant asks the god for forgiveness with folded hands. Carvings inside the temple portray the story of this epic battle.

The Dark Rocks of the Deccan

Nearly 65–68 million years ago, long before the first human beings walked the earth, volcanic eruptions shook parts of the land that now make up the western and central regions of the Indian subcontinent. At that time, the Indian plate was still located way below the equator and had not yet joined the Eurasian plate. The erupted lava spread across expansive portions of the region, over present-day Gujarat, Maharashtra and Madhya Pradesh. The lava eventually cooled and solidified into stair-like, dark basalt layers known as 'traps', thus forming what we call the Deccan Traps today. Basalt is a type of rock formed by volcanoes.

Some geologists believe that a giant meteor struck the earth, setting off a number of volcanic eruptions around the planet – even the ones around the Indian plate's western and central regions. Smoke and gases rising from these flaming volcanoes changed the planet's temperature. All of this led to mass extinction on earth, including that of the dinosaurs!

An Explosive Phenomenon

The landscape of Lonar in Maharashtra's Buldhana district also falls in the ancient volcanic region of the Deccan Traps. More than 50,000 years ago, when a meteor struck this very spot, the Lonar impact crater – the largest hypervelocity basaltic crater on earth – was formed. As the time period suggests, this meteoric strike was different from that of the giant meteor which is believed to have caused volcanic eruptions and the Deccan Traps millions of years ago.

When a meteor or an asteroid, moving at an extremely high speed, crashes into another surface, the impact is very much like an explosion. *Kaboom!* This is called a hypervelocity impact. The large hollow of Lonar was created when a meteor, travelling at a speed of around 90,000 kilometres per hour, struck the earth. As groundwater and rainfall filled it up, the crater was transformed into a lake.

Moody Microbes

Lonasura may or may not exist in the lake, but experts think that the meteor that caused the impact crater might still be lying at the bottom. Maskelynite, a rare glass-like mineral found on some meteors, has been found on stones and rocks near the lake.

The water in the crater has been of interest to scientists as well. Usually turquoise green (a colour that the lake gets from the various types of algae growing in it), the lake's water suddenly turned pinkish red in June 2020. Was the injured Lonasura really living in it? Scientists realized that as the lake's water level went down in the summer, its salinity, or salt levels, went up. This led to the breeding of haloarchaea, a microbe that produces a pinkish pigment. When the monsoon set in and the water level increased, the salt levels and the microbe numbers reduced. This gradually changed the water's colour back to its original hue. That's some incredible magic!

The blow dealt by Daitya Sudan formed a large crater in Lonar. But did you know that a goddess and her sisters once created hundreds of small craters?

24

A Goddess's Work of Art

Nighoj

'We're doomed,' one of the gods whispered.

'Yes, no one can save us now,' another lamented softly.

'Be quiet! Have some faith in Shankara,' a third admonished.

Although they were almost inaudible, Shiva had heard every word. As he closed his eyes and thought about the problem they now faced, he could only hear the sound of the Ganga flowing through the half-knot of his hair. He opened his eyes and smiled.

Deva Lok was cacophonous that day. All thirty-three crore gods had assembled to meet Shiva (whom some of them called Shankara). As soon as Shiva arrived for the meeting, some of the gods cried in one voice: 'O Shankara, you have to help us.'

Shiva raised his hand, gesturing them to calm down. 'What is the matter?' he asked.

'O Shankara,' one of the gods said, 'the demon Dhumraksha has become a huge threat to all the worlds. You have to take away his powers or defeat him in battle!'

The others started clamouring loudly as well.

'Please, stop. Let me think,' Shiva requested. He knew that no male god could defeat Dhumraksha because of a boon. So, he turned to his wife, Parvati. 'Devi, would you please...' he began, but before he could complete his request, she held up a hand.

'I would have, but I have fought so many asuras recently I think I deserve some rest. Even if I agree to fight, in my present state, Dhumraksha will be difficult to beat!'

Parvati was right. Dhumraksha had indeed grown very strong. The disheartened gods began talking among themselves again.

Shiva tried to shut out all the noise by focusing on his breath. When he heard the gurgling sound of Ganga's waters, he asked her, 'Goddess, will you please...'

Before he could complete his request, Ganga replied, 'Sure!'

The goddess took on the form of a young child to fight the deadly demon. Shiva named her new avatar Malganga.

To win the battle, Malganga created six sisters who were as young and as powerful as her. Armed with the best weapons and accompanied by her sisters and an army of thirty-three crore gods, Malganga descended to Prithvi Lok.

As the large divine army marched towards Dhumraksha's palace, the earth trembled. Wondering what had caused the quake, Dhumraksha peeped out of the balcony of his royal chambers.

'You! Out!' Malganga snapped, standing outside his palace.

The asura was taken aback. 'A chit of a girl talking to me like that!' Dhumraksha growled.

Noticing some familiar faces in the army, Dhumraksha realized that they were there to wage war. Soon, his palace gates opened, and crores of asura warriors poured out. The thirty-three crore gods and the seven sisters had a busy time wiping out Dhumraksha's forces.

Malganga then fought the demon single-handedly. She was quicker than lightning.

'Where did that girl go again?' Dhumraksha wondered. He was stronger than many of the gods in the army for sure, but he was a bit too slow for Malganga's sudden strikes. He only huffed and puffed, unable to match her speed.

The girl finally shot a divine arrow at Dhumraksha. He didn't even see it coming. Gravely wounded, he fell to his knees. 'Who are you?' he asked, trembling.

'I am Malganga, an avatar of Ganga,' she said.

Dhumraksha smiled at his foolishness. 'I'm happy to have been defeated by a warrior–goddess like you!' The exhausted asura lay down on the ground and breathed his last.

After the battle, the gods were tired too. They decided to rest at a serene, secluded spot on Prithvi Lok for a while. As they reached the banks of a raging river, Malganga instantly fell in love with its beauty. 'Here!' she said, gesturing everybody to stop.

Later, as Malganga and her sisters bathed in the river, they realized that something was not quite right. 'The waters are too fast,' one of the sisters said, trying to hold on to the rocks so she wouldn't be swept away.

'I agree. We must control its flow and balance its currents,' another sister suggested.

Malganga nodded. She started carving circular, pot-like hollows in the river's rocky banks with her fingernails. After observing her for a few minutes, her sisters joined in as well.

In a single night, Malganga and her sisters managed to carve hundreds of magnificent craters and holes. The water began flowing in a complex pattern now – cascading over a slope, falling into and out of multiple zigzag potholes, and finally flowing back into the river's course in a much calmer manner a little ahead.

'Better,' Malganga said, watching the flow of the river.

The divine army had planned to stay at this spot for only a few days. But the days turned into weeks and

months, until Malganga announced one morning, 'I want to stay here forever!'

'So do we!' her sisters chorused, and they picked different spots along the riverbank to reside in.

'We'll stay with you too!' said the thirty-three crore gods, and each of them took on the form of a tamarind tree.

Eventually, the entire divine army transformed into a large tamarind grove that flourished near the river. The lush setting attracted several species of birds, especially peafowl.

Listening to the melodious birdcalls and watching the river dancing through the potholes, Malganga felt completely at peace.

'Home!' she sighed happily.

Connecting the Dots...

The fierce river along which Malganga and her sisters settled is the Kukadi – it flows through Maharashtra between Nighoj, a village in Ahmednagar's Parner taluka, and Takli Haji, a village in Pune's Shirur taluka. On its banks are hundreds of pot-like hollows. It is believed that Malganga and her sisters live here even today, in the temples built for them by devotees along the riverbank. Near Nighoj is a village named Morachi Chincholi, which gets its name from the numerous peacocks found prancing around and the tamarind trees growing there.

The Water Kettles

The Kukadi houses Asia's largest natural riverine pothole formations on its banks. (These are very different from the potholes you see on the roads during the monsoon!) Riverine potholes are simply pot-shaped holes that form along a river's banks. The ones along the Kukadi are made of black basaltic rock as this unique landscape is part of the Deccan Traps that formed millions of years ago.

The 'giant kettles', as these potholes are also known, are usually formed by smaller rocks or pebbles. Washed away by turbulent waters, smaller rocks and pebbles settle in the cracks of rocky riverbanks. Then, they move through the tiny cracks in a circular manner due to the action of flowing water. As they keep swirling under the currents for hundreds and thousands of years, they slowly chip away at the edges of these cracks, making them bigger and bigger, until they eventually look like bowls or potholes. Because of the continuous churning, the pebbles and the potholes end up having a smooth surface. At Nighoj too, smooth, circular pebbles can be seen inside many of the potholes.

Due to these formations, the Kukadi seems to follow a zigzag or disorderly course, flowing in and out of these potholes and gaps. As a result of many twists, turns and breaks in its path, the waters that gush forcefully on one side can be seen flowing calmly on the other side, just a little ahead.

The goddess, her sisters and the thirty-three crore gods made the Kukadi and its banks more beautiful than it already was. But today, picknickers and tourists do not seem to respect the hollows in the way they revere the goddess. Not only do they leave behind graffiti on the basaltic rock surfaces, but they also regularly dump litter inside the potholes. Perhaps the goddess chooses to appear every year as a grey-brown pot then (which somewhat resembles the riverine potholes) just to remind people that she's still living among them?

The Vessel in the Well

When Malganga had first come to Nighoj, she was a young girl. Years later, after she grew up, she decided to live in a sacred well, which was built near her temple. Her devotees believe that she appears to them every year in the form of a vessel.

Lakhs of devotees visit the sacred well at Nighoj between March and April each year to witness the miracle. Earlier, Malganga used to appear as a golden or copper pot. However, a devotee once stole the utensil which had magically appeared in the well. From then on, Malganga has emerged as an earthen vessel instead!

Malganga and her sisters altered the flow and the speed of the Kukadi River. But did you know that a divine being once partially changed the temperature of another river?

25

All for Parvati's Earring

Manikaran

'Shesha, only *you* can stop Shiva now!' Goddess Naina said to the giant thousand-headed snake. 'Please return Parvati's gem!'

The divine serpent's gaze was fixed on Shiva. The god was still doing the *taandav*, a dance he usually broke into when he was very, very angry.

The earth shook violently. Parvati and Shiva's followers looked on helplessly at the dancing god. Without responding to Naina, Sheshnag watched the *taandav* for some more time and then dived back into the waters from which he had emerged. He swam deep below and reached his home in Patal Lok. His several pairs of eyes intently scoured the Chamber of Precious Gems in his abode.

'There must be millions of gems here,' Sheshnag wondered aloud. 'But which one of these belongs to Parvati?'

Once, while strolling through a mountainous region, Parvati and Shiva came upon a beautiful land. Parvati was quite taken by the foaming river that ran through it. The couple decided to stay there for a while. Time flew so fast that they ended up staying there for more than 1,100 years!

One morning, while Parvati was bathing as usual in the gushing river, the precious *mani* or gem from one of her earrings fell into the water.

'Oh no, that gem is irreplaceable!' she cried.

'Don't look so sad, Parvati. I'll ask my followers to look for it,' Shiva told her.

Shiva's followers looked everywhere – they even swam down to the riverbed and searched it thoroughly, despite the fast-flowing waters. But the precious stone was nowhere to be seen! Drenched to their bones, their failure clearly visible on their faces, they approached Shiva, who flew into a rage.

'One gem! So many of you could not find one single *gem*?' Shiva thundered. His followers didn't say anything – they knew it was wise to keep quiet when the god was angry.

Shiva then addressed the entire universe, 'Whoever has the gem, better return it *now*.' He struck his *trishul* into the ground.

Even though he was extremely angry, Shiva waited for the gem to be returned. But no one came forward. Finally, having completely lost his patience, he opened his third eye. From the flames that emanated from this eye, Goddess Naina appeared.

Shiva then began performing the *taandav*, the dance of destruction. Naina looked worried. In her mind's eye, she saw where the gem was. Through a gap in the riverbed, the gem had fallen further down and landed in Patal Lok. And there, Sheshnag had happily tossed it away onto one of the many heaps of *mani*s that adorned his Chamber of Precious Gems.

'Oh no!' Naina exclaimed, and quickly went down to Patal Lok to talk to Sheshnag.

'All for a gem?' the amused serpent king asked Naina.

'It's not any gem, Shesha. It's a *mani* from *Parvati*'s earring,' the goddess pointed out.

Wanting to witness Shiva's affection for his wife himself, which was on full display through his dance of destruction, Sheshnag rose out of the river and watched the *taandav* for a while. When Naina pleaded with him again, the divine serpent returned to his abode to fetch the gem.

Back home, he stared at the huge mounds of precious stones that lay in front of him, utterly confused. At last, he had an idea.

Rising out of the waters once again, Sheshnag hissed loudly. From his thousand mouths, he spewed a shower of precious gems, each one a different colour and a different size. The warmth of his breath, as he hissed

and spat out the stones, turned that part of the icy river into boiling hot water.

As the steaming water bubbled wildly, Sheshnag called out to Shiva and Parvati, 'I've brought you all the gems I had in Patal Lok. Please pick the one that belongs to you.'

Even from a distance, Parvati could spot her beloved gem. 'That one!' she exclaimed and ran towards it. She picked it up, attached it to her earring and beamed. Shiva, who had stopped dancing by now, smiled at Parvati affectionately.

The boiling waters, however, remained a part of the raging river. Shiva travelled a little distance away, and sat on the banks of the same stream, where the waters were still freezing cold. Shutting his eyes, he began to meditate. Everything was calm once again, and the universe continued to thrum with life.

Connecting the Dots...

The valley where the divine couple had lived for more than a millennium is known today as the Parvati Valley. It is situated in the Kullu district of Himachal Pradesh. The river where the goddess lost the precious stone is also named after her. The part of the River Parvati where the waters turned hot is known as the Manikaran Hot Springs. In Sanskrit, karan *or* karn *means 'ear' and so,* manikaran *means 'precious earring'.*

It is said that for several centuries, people who visited the Manikaran Hot Springs found gems and stones on its riverbed. However, after an earthquake occurred in the region in 1905, the appearance of gems stopped mysteriously. Did Sheshnag shake things up a bit and take his stones back to Patal Lok?

A Bubbling Boon

Guru Nanak, the founder of the faith Sikhism, once reached the banks of a frothy river in Kullu along with his companions Bhai Mardana and Bhai Bala. They had travelled for a long time, and this seemed to be a good spot for a break.

'What's the matter? You look pensive,' Guru Nanak asked Bhai Mardana as they settled on the riverbank.

'I'm a bit hungry,' he replied.

'Let's get a few ingredients from the locals and prepare a meal then,' Guru Nanak suggested.

Bhai Mardaṇa brought back flour, which was offered by some generous locals, and prepared some dough. That's when he realized that there was a small problem. 'Now that the dough for the chapatis is ready, how and where do we cook them?' he asked.

Guru Nanak smiled and lifted a large stone that lay nearby. To the astonishment of Bhai Mardana and Bhai Bala, there was a spring of bubbling hot water underneath. 'Here!' Guru Nanak said.

Bhai Mardana immersed pieces of the rolled-out dough into the steaming water. But each time, they sank. He looked at Guru Nanak and shook his head.

Guru Nanak had the answer to this problem too: 'You've missed the most important ingredient – gratitude!'

So, the trio closed their eyes and prayed, 'O Supreme Being, thank you for the flour and the gift of this hot spring. We offer you what we have. Help us cook the food and serve you.'

After this, Bhai Mardana tried to cook the rolled-out dough in the boiling water again. This time, the chapatis that he slowly slipped in not only floated, but they also cooked well. Thrilled, the three of them enjoyed a hot meal, watching the cool waters of the river run past them.

Connecting the Dots...

The waterbody next to which Guru Nanak, Bhai Mardana and Bhai Bala rested was the River Parvati and the boiling waters revealed by Guru Nanak were the Manikaran Hot Springs. This event is said to have occurred in 1574. A Sikh shrine called Manikaran Gurdwara now stands at the very spot where Bhai Mardana had cooked the meal.

The Fountainhead

Hundreds of hot springs exist in India, and Manikaran is amongst the most well known of them. Often, spouts of boiling water exist in the middle, or at one end, of a river that otherwise carries cool water. This happens because the groundwater in those areas is heated underground and pushed up due to geothermal pressure.

The heat produced under the earth's surface is called geothermal heat, and the pressure caused by this heat is called geothermal pressure. The inner parts of the earth are made up of solid and liquid layers containing molten rocks. When groundwater comes close to these molten rocks beneath the earth, the water is heated and pushed up due to pressure.

Just as an erupting volcano throws up pieces of hot rock, geothermally heated water too erupts through cracks and gaps in the earth's surface, in the form of a hot water spring. This is why hot springs are also known as thermal springs.

A Wellspring of Goodness

A great source of green energy, hot water springs can be harnessed to generate geothermal power or electricity. And they are popular among tourists for their healing effects.

The chemical and mineral content of water gives thermal springs essential medicinal properties. While most Indian hot springs contain large amounts of sulphur (a yellowish chemical substance), Manikaran is known for its high levels of uranium (a greyish radioactive substance). Often, people with disorders related to the nervous system, bones, muscles and the skin bathe in thermal springs to cure themselves or find relief from pain.

Apart from being utilized for their medicinal value, the water from hot springs can indeed be used for cooking!

A Water-Cooked Meal

The traditional community kitchen run by Sikh volunteers and the meals they prepare there which are freely served to the hungry are together called *langar*. Even today, the Manikaran Gurdwara's *langar* is prepared in the same bubbling spring. Pots of rice are covered with a clean, damp cloth and placed in the waters. The chapatis are still prepared in the same way as Bhai Mardana had made them centuries ago – by slipping rolled-out dough into the water and pulling them out once they are cooked!

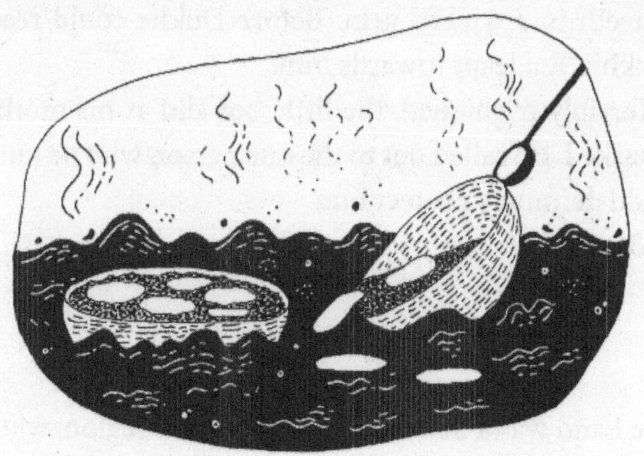

Sheshnag created a distinct pool of hot water in the otherwise chilly Parvati River. But did you know that a young goddess once divided a unique forest into two separate zones?

26
The Land of Tides and Tigers
Sundarbans

Dukhe knew it was no use trying to run away because Dokkhin Rai was extremely fast. As he wiped his tears, the boy saw Dokkhin Rai transform into a tiger.

'I'm going to eat you now,' the beast leered, baring his teeth in a wicked grin. Before Dukhe could react, Dokkhin Rai leapt towards him.

Terribly frightened, the little boy did as his mother had asked. He called out to the one person who he knew would definitely protect him.

'Bonbibiiiii!'

Tide Land was a marshy, thickly forested region, where water from the nearby sea entered and exited at will all through the year. It was made up of many little islands, with water channels cutting criss-cross patterns through them. Dokkhin Rai was the king of the forest in Tide Land. The trees and the woods, the beehives and the honey, the mudbanks and the crabs – all of these belonged to him alone.

When humans began to inhabit this land, they began using the resources of the forest freely. Not all humans were the same – some collected only what they required, while others greedily took more from the woods.

Dokkhin Rai didn't like this one bit. He was also a human being, but he was unlike everyone else. He had a supernatural power – he could turn himself into a tiger! So, one day, when he'd finally had enough, Dokkhin Rai decided to use this superpower and demand a human sacrifice from every group that entered the woods. This way, he began sowing the seed of fear among Tide Land's human inhabitants.

The tiger king's biggest support was his mother, Narayani. She too believed that the forest belonged solely to her son. Unchallenged, his power made him more arrogant with each passing day. In time, he became so evil that he transformed into a demon king. The mere mention of his name sent shivers down the spine of anyone who wanted to venture into the forest. They knew that Rai Thakur, as he was also known, would not let a group go home without killing one of them.

It was then that Allah decided to put an end to this reign of terror. He chose a young girl, who also lived in Tide Land, for this task.

'My child, I want you to protect Tide Land from the dread of Dokkhin Rai,' His voice called out to the girl from the skies.

Along with her twin brother, Shah Jongali, the girl headed straight to the forest. There, she challenged the demon king, 'Oi, Dokkhin Rai, Shah Jongali and I have come to test your powers. Fight us with all your might!'

Dokkhin Rai was about to pounce on them, but Narayani stopped him. 'Let *me* fight the young lady first!' she cried.

A long battle followed. When Narayani realized that she couldn't win, she surrendered.

'O Bonbibi, lady of the forest,' she said. 'From now on you are my sister. I promise, Dokkhin Rai won't harm anyone who worships you.' Bonbibi was happy with this truce.

The news of this fight spread throughout Tide Land. In Bonbibi, the inhabitants had found a new hero. Encouraged by the fact that Dokkhin Rai wouldn't harm anyone now, Dhonai, a wealthy man in Tide Land, devised an elaborate plan to go deep into the forest to collect honey. Seven large boats were readied for the journey. Due to its marshy location and the perennial flooding, the people of Tide Land had to use boats to travel from one place to another.

Dhonai's brother, Monai, warned him against this plan. 'We already have so much, Brother. Why do you want more honey? Seven boats full of men! Isn't that a bit much? You're going to stoke Dokkhin Rai's wrath.'

'Don't lecture me. I am going to look for one more person to complete my team,' Dhonai said and walked off.

In one of the villages of Tide Land, Dhonai found Dukhe, the young son of a widow. 'If you join me in this journey, you and your mother can lead a happy, comfortable life – free of all worries,' he told the child.

'I'll surely come with you, Chacha!' the innocent boy said.

But Dukhe's mother was afraid to let him go. With tears in her eyes, she instructed him, 'If you come face to face with Dokkhin Rai, pray to Bonbibi.'

Later, deep inside the forest, just as Monai had feared, Dokkhin Rai was furious to see Dhonai and his large crew.

'You thought you could get away without sacrificing a member of your team?' Dokkhin Rai asked angrily, suddenly appearing in front of them.

'Let the boy be my meal, and take all the honey you want,' he said, suddenly noticing Dukhe.

'How can I let you have this child, Rai Thakur?' a shocked Dhonai said.

But Dokkhin Rai was adamant. Realizing that the demon king could turn himself into a tiger at any moment now, Dhonai left poor Dukhe behind. The men then returned to their boats. Shivering with fright, Dukhe hid behind the large trunk of a sundari tree. Just as Dokkhin Rai was about to tear Dukhe apart with his claws, the boy called upon Bonbibi.

A blinding light forced Dokkhin Rai to move away from Dukhe. From that light, Bonbibi and Shah Jongali emerged.

'I'll get him!' Shah Jongali said, twirling his mighty mace, chasing Dokkhin Rai further into the woods.

Dokkhin Rai rushed to his friend, Pir Gazi. 'Gazi, please let me hide here. Shah Jongali is coming for me. He won't leave me alive,' he pleaded.

Pir Gazi, a saint who lived in Tide Land, spent much of his time with the tigers in the jungle.

'Why, what have you done now? I thought it was all settled between you and the twins?' he asked. The other tigers who were sitting around the saint moved to make way as he walked towards Dokkhin Rai.

Just then, Shah Jongali, Bonbibi and Dukhe reached Pir Gazi's camp. Before Shah Jongali could attack Dokkhin Rai, Pir Gazi quickly advised the tiger king, 'Apologize, Dokkhin Rai. Promise them that you will never hunt any human who enters the forest.'

Dokkhin Rai apologized but refused to make that promise. 'If I do that, then people's greed will know no bounds. And if I don't protect my forest, it will be destroyed.'

'Dokkhin Rai is right,' a voice agreed.

Much to everyone's surprise, it was Bonbibi who had spoken. 'The forest is as much Dokkhin Rai's as

it is ours. The tigers belong here as much as we do. If tigers kill and eat humans without control, they are greedy. But if humans take more from the forest than they should, they are greedy too.'

'But Bonbibi, this is a never-ending conflict,' Shah Jongali said.

'Yes, and that is why we must accept each other as family – the tigers, the people, Dokkhin Rai, Shah Jongali, Dukhe, Pir Gazi and I. Let's divide this forest...some part of it for the humans and some for the wildlife. Neither group should be greedy and cross their limits,' she suggested.

'That's a great solution,' Pir Gazi said, happy that Dokkhin Rai's life had been spared.

'But for the trauma that you've caused this child, you have to gift him enough honey to end his poverty,' Bonbibi told Dokkhin Rai, patting Dukhe's head affectionately.

Dokkhin Rai readily agreed. Laden with pots and pots of honey, Dukhe went home sitting on the back of a crocodile.

Ever since, the people of Tide Land have lived in the zones allocated to them. Bonbibi continues to protect them when they go into the jungle to collect wood and honey. There, however, Dokkhin Rai keeps a keen, watchful eye on the humans, lest anyone turn greedy and exploit his forest.

Connecting the Dots...

Today, Tide Land is known as the Sundarbans Mangrove Forest. After Bangladesh became a separate country in 1971, nearly sixty per cent of the Sundarbans was included within the country's border. The remaining forty per cent is located in West Bengal, adjacent to the Bay of Bengal.

For many communities in India, the geography of the place they inhabit determines their chief occupations and means of livelihood. In the Sundarbans too, the professions of local inhabitants are closely connected to the forest around them – they are honey collectors, woodcutters, crab collectors and fisherfolk. They live in constant fear of the tigers that roam through the forested areas.

Honey collectors are the most cautious of all, as they need to go deep inside the woods to find honey. They recite the Bonbibi Johurnama, *a text that details Bonbibi's story, throughout their journey into the forest. They also pray to Dokkhin Rai – especially before touching the beehive – as they believe that he is the creator of honey.*

The Tiger Tamers

In Islam, pir is a title given to warrior saints. Pir Gazi, in this story, is believed to represent the warrior saints who came to this region in the twelfth or thirteenth century to spread the teachings of Islam. They not only cleared portions of the mangrove forest for farmlands and homes for those who agreed to settle here, but are also said to have succeeded in taming the wildlife. Ancient scroll paintings from Bengal have depicted Pir Gazi as a warrior saint, riding on the back of a tiger.

The Fragmented Forest

The Sundarbans Mangrove Forest is not exactly a single mass of land. It consists of multiple water channels, mudflats and mangrove islands. At present, the Indian Sundarbans includes 102 islands. Of these, 54 are inhabited. The remaining are untouched, wild mangrove jungles. Together, all of the islands make the Sundarbans the largest mangrove forest and estuarine delta in the world.

Believe it or not, the formation of the Sundarbans is actually connected to the Himalayas!

When the snow melts in the Himalayan mountain ranges, it flows down in the form of rivers. Three such rivers – the Ganga, the Brahmaputra and the Meghna – travel from the Himalayas towards the Bay of Bengal. The waters of these rivers bring with them a large amount of silt (sediment), which remains at the estuary – the part where these rivers meet the Bay of Bengal. This site, where multiple tracts of sediments branch out at the estuary, is known as a delta. Freshwater comes into the Sundarbans through the three rivers, while the Bay of Bengal brings in saline or salty water.

The Ebb and Flow of Nature's Powers

The landscape of the Sundarbans changes continuously due to the action of high and low tides – the rising and receding water levels in the Bay of Bengal. The mangrove forest is thus prone to frequent flooding and receding of its waters. As a result of this, numerous tracts or belts of a tidal delta have been formed at the estuary over the years, making it look like the disjointed pieces of a jigsaw puzzle. This is why the Sundarbans is also called Tide Land.

Tides are caused by the positions of the sun, moon and the earth. The gravitational pull of the moon makes the water levels surge on the side of the earth that faces it, while water levels recede on the opposite side of the planet, which is away from the moon. So, if the moon causes a high tide in the region that is facing it, a low tide is caused on the other side of the earth.

A Wild and Wonderful World

The swamps of the Sundarbans are home to some fascinating animals: the saltwater crocodile (the largest crocodile species in the world), the water monitor lizard (one of the largest monitor lizard species in the world) and the mudskipper (an amphibious fish species that not only skips out of the water onto the wet mud, but also climbs the mangrove trees!).

The world's largest mangrove forest is also the abode of the Royal Bengal tigers. The tigers of the Sundarbans have adapted well to its unusual geography and saline ecosystem – they are expert swimmers and feed on fish and crabs (apart from other wildlife). They also have a reputation of being man-eaters.

Conservationists are constantly finding new ways to keep the prowling big cats and humans away from each other. But locals believe that even today, only praying to Bonbibi and Dokkhin Rai can protect them. The legend of Bonbibi highlights this tiger-human conflict, which is an inevitable part of the Sundarbans.

A Mark of Character

The Sundarbans is dotted with walled or thatched shrines dedicated to Bonbibi, housing idols of the goddess, Shah Jongali, Dokkhin Rai, Dukhe and Pir Gazi.

In Bangla, *ban* or *bon* (pronounced 'bawn') means 'forest'; so, Bonbibi means 'lady of the forest'. But since *bon* (when pronounced 'bone') means 'sister', Bonbibi could also mean 'the lady considered a sister'. Remember what Narayani said to the goddess after their battle?

Dokkhin means 'the south', and *rai* means 'king'. Dokkhin Rai is the 'king of the southern region', which is said to be the tigers' domain in Sundarbans in real life.

Shah means 'ruler', and *jongali* means 'of the jungle'; so, Shah Jongali is the 'ruler of the jungle'.

Dukhe gets his name from *dukkha*, meaning 'sadness' or 'misery'.

Dhonai's name comes from *dhan* ('wealth'), while that of Monai comes from *mana* ('mind').

Sundar means 'beautiful'; so, Sundarbans means 'beautiful forest'. It gets its name from a mangrove species that grows there – the *Heritiera fomes*, locally called sundari.

To minimize conflict, Bonbibi set boundaries for humans and wildlife in the Sundarbans. But did you know that there was another mangrove forest where the limits of divine powers and human abilities were tested?

27

The Stage for the Dance of Delight

Pichavaram

'Hah, what will you do now?' the chief sage asked. 'How will you face the great asura Muyalakan?'

The mendicant smiled, slowly struck a dance pose and said, 'Watch me!'

The asura burst into full-throated laughter. 'What is this? A dance competition?'

Without responding, the mendicant began dancing.

'Hey you! What do you think you're doing?' the chief sage asked.

'Oh, he's just trying to distract us,' Muyalakan said, and began hopping towards his dancing opponent.

Midway, he realized that the mendicant's graceful dance had suddenly turned vigorous and dynamic. The ground trembled and Muyalakan lost his balance and rolled over. Then, the mendicant did something that made the sages gasp.

Thillai Vanam was a thick forest, covered with knotty mangroves. It was far away from civilization, and not many knew of its existence.

Once, a group of sages accidentally found their way into Thillai Vanam. Years of penance had given them magical powers that had made them proud and vain. The ambitious sages now wanted to acquire more supernatural knowledge. To do this, they had to perform a series of rituals in the utmost secrecy. The mangrove forest seemed like the perfect setting for their secret rituals, as no outsiders could ever find their way in and disturb them. So, the sages decided to settle there, along with their families.

One morning, as they sat around the sacred fire for a ritual, the chief sage said, 'Isn't it funny how we manipulate and control the gods by chanting holy verses and using our magical powers?'

'Doesn't that make *us* more powerful than the gods we worship?' a young sage asked. The others nodded in agreement and laughed.

The discussion went on for a while, with each sage recalling various rituals and the effects they had had on different gods.

From behind some bushes, a mendicant, who had somehow managed to navigate his way through the dense forest, watched them and listened to their conversation intently. He smiled and said to himself, 'Let's have some fun with these *powerful* sages!' He waited until the sages had begun conducting their ritual and were lost in prayer. Then, he emerged and slowly approached their homes.

'Would you care to feed a hungry soul?' he called out, standing outside the chief sage's hut.

The wife of the chief sage came out of her home, puzzled to discover that someone had reached their remote habitation.

'How did you find your way here?' she asked. As she looked at him, she was mesmerized by his handsome face.

Seeing her in a trance, another sage's wife rushed to see what was going on. She froze as well and began staring at the mendicant. Slowly, one by one, the wives of all the sages gathered around; he was like a magnet, drawing them out of their homes towards him.

Distracted by what was going on near their homes, a little distance away from the sacred fire, the chief sage stopped his chant mid-verse and threw an angry glance at his wife.

But she barely noticed. 'You have such a charming aura. Who are you?' she gushed to the stranger.

'Yes, we've never seen you here before,' another lady said.

'Enough!' the chief sage thundered, getting to his feet. 'Go inside,' he yelled at his wife and the other women. But they didn't move. Only when the mendicant himself gestured them to move, did they go back into their respective homes.

'What sorcery have you performed on them?' the chief sage asked, seeing that the mendicant had trapped the women in a trance.

'All of you think you can control the gods, so I thought I'd show off some of my magical powers too,' the mendicant replied.

'Not only have you trespassed into our area, but you have also been eavesdropping. You will pay for this. You will surely pay for this!' the furious chief sage shouted.

'And *how* will you punish me? By chanting some gibberish? Using your phony powers?'

'How *dare* you?' The enraged sage drew an invisible magical sign mid-air. Venomous serpents appeared out of nowhere and flew towards the mendicant.

But the latter calmly caught each of them, twirling this way and that, as if he were dancing, and wore them on his arms, wrists and ankles as ornaments. Strangely, the snakes did him no harm, but hissed violently at the sages instead.

Another sage then chanted some verses, gritting his teeth. A gigantic tiger emerged from the sacred fire. Roaring ferociously, the beast leapt towards the mendicant. But he caught the tiger with his bare hands, and pirouetted thrice with such speed that the sages only saw a whirl of dust.

When he finally stood still, they were astounded. The animal had vanished into thin air. Only the tiger's skin remained, which the mendicant had wrapped around his waist as a skirt.

'You like that?' the mendicant winked at the stunned sages.

Each of the other sages tried to defeat this unlikely opponent through their magic, but in vain.

Finally, they formed a large circle around the sacred fire, and began to chant verses in unison and draw signs in the air. A mighty asura appeared suddenly – short and stout, he looked and hopped much like a hare.

'Muyalakan, destroy him!' the sages ordered him.

It was while fighting this hare-like asura that the mendicant began dancing. His tied-up, matted hair flew open. He twirled and jumped high in the air, plucking a handful of *thillai* leaves growing nearby and wore them as his crown.

The mendicant's dynamic dance shook the earth, making Muyalakan lose his balance and roll over. At that moment, he jumped onto the asura's back.

Pressing his right foot down to pin Muyalakan to the ground, he lifted his left leg up, across his right leg. His two arms transformed into four! While the two hands at the back held a *damaru* and fire, the hands in the front struck a dancing pose.

A standing ring of flames appeared around him. 'Control me now with your chants and powers,' the transformed mendicant said.

The stunned sages and Muyalakan let out a gasp, awed by the new avatar.

The chief sage fell to his knees, raised his arms towards the stranger and began to sing:

'It is he who manifests as all five elements of nature
It is he – the past, present and the future,
It is he who wears the *thillai* as his crown,
It is he who has brought Muyalakan down,
It is he who has taken the all-powerful cosmic stance,
It is he – Nataraja, the king of dance
It is he who has staged the *aananda taandava*
It is he – the Mahadeva…Shiva!'

And that is how Shiva, appearing as a mendicant, taught the sages a lesson in humility.

Connecting the Dots...

The lush region, where this entire episode played out, is known today as the Pichavaram Mangrove Forest. It lies close to Chidambaram, a town in the Cuddalore district, Tamil Nadu. Excoecaria agallocha (thillai *in Tamil) is a kind of mangrove plant found in abundance in Pichavaram and so, the forest is also called Thillai Vanam, or '*thillai *forest'.*

It is said that Pichavaram has receded by many kilometres over the past few millennia. Not so surprisingly, around 14 kilometres away from this forest, in Chidambaram town, now stands a famous Shiva temple called the Thillai Nataraja Temple – since he wore a crown of thillai *leaves, he is worshipped as Thillai Nataraja.*

Some people believe that Chidambaram gets its name from the words chithu *and* aambalam, *meaning the 'dance of the god' and 'stage' respectively – this suggests that Chidambaram is the very site or the stage where Shiva had performed his dance of delight.*

Another view is that the name Chidambaram is derived from the Tamil words chit *and* ambaram, *which mean 'consciousness' and 'sky' respectively. The temple at Chidambaram is one of five important Shiva shrines in the country, each of which represents one of the five natural elements. Among them, the temple at Chidambaram stands for 'ether' or 'sky'.*

The Hunter and the Hare

Nataraja and Muyalakan share an intriguing connection with the stars and astronomy. The constellation Orion is said to look like a hunter who is chasing the Lepus constellation of stars, which resembles a hare. Mythologists say that Nataraja is a representation of Orion, while Muyalakan is a symbol of Lepus. This comparison does not seem far-fetched because Muyalakan gets his name from the Tamil word *muyal*, which means 'hare'.

The asura Muyalakan is also seen as a representation of epilepsy – a neurological disorder that causes seizures (convulsions, abnormal muscle movements and a loss of consciousness). Studies show that different parts of the plant *excoecaria agallocha* or *thillai* have therapeutic effects. In fact, in some parts of the world, *thillai* leaves are also used to treat epilepsy. The striking image of Thillai Nataraja, with his leafy crown, subduing Muyalakan makes perfect sense now, doesn't it?

The Waterside Grove

Pichavaram is a mangrove ecosystem covering more than 1,000 hectares. Consisting of 50-plus islands and hundreds of water canals, it is the second-largest mangrove wetland in the world.

A wetland, as the term suggests, is an area that is surrounded by water from a lake, river, sea or floods. The vegetation that grows over a wetland depends on the kind of water that flows through or surrounds it. A mangrove wetland includes a mangrove forest as well as the waterbodies around it. Such wetlands occur in coastal areas and have saline or salty water coming in from the sea. Pichavaram too, a mangrove wetland, is situated near the country's south-eastern coast, in Tamil Nadu, alongside the Bay of Bengal.

Mangroves prevent soil erosion and act as a barricade against destruction during storms and floods. They also reduce the damage caused by earthquakes by absorbing seismic waves or shock waves. Despite their many benefits, mangrove forests, including the one at Pichavaram, have been cut down for various reasons. The protection of this wetland is especially important because many species of mangrove trees and plants have medicinal properties. For example, the *thillai* plant (*excoecaria agallocha*) can also be used for pain management and in the treatment of diabetes, cancer and more. Thankfully, conservation efforts, such as the creation of new canals and water pathways, are set to improve water circulation and mangrove growth at Pichavaram.

The Dance of the Universe

Pichavaram is considered to be a gift from Pichatanandar, the mendicant form of Shiva. Just as the mangrove forest guards many green secrets, the form of Nataraja (which Pichatanandar assumes in the end) also contains certain hidden messages. For this especially, it is highly revered by artists, sculptors and dancers across India.

The *taandav*, which Shiva performs when he is angry, is called the 'dance of destruction'. Whereas he performs the *aananda taandav*, or the 'dance of delight', when he is in a happy mood. In the Nataraja pose, which is a part of this happy dance, his upper right hand, which holds the *damaru*, a small drum, represents the creation of the universe; the lower right hand, which blesses everyone, stands for preservation. The upper left hand, holding fire, represents destruction. The god's right leg, standing over Muyalakan, represents a lack of knowledge or the disregard for it (the very qualities that Muyalakan and the sages exhibited in their pride). His raised left leg stands for freedom from such qualities that hold people down.

The ring of fire around the dancing god stands for the cosmos or universe, while his composite stance (which is famously called the Nataraja pose) embodies the movement of the universe.

By overpowering the arrogant sages and the asura, Nataraja teaches us that the universe is indeed supreme – be it in the realms of mythology, science, cosmology or geography!

Pause and Play

The world that Brahma built, and the land's sudden tilt,
Vishnu's big victory, and the stone arch's history,
Shiva's sparkling crown, and the glacier's melting down,
Matsya's search for refuge, and the fury of a deluge,
Jalodbhava's refusal to budge, and the *karewas*' layers of sludge,
Parashurama's aim so fine, and the appearance of a coastline,
Vasuki's still gaze, and the *sarpa kaavu*'s green ways,
Krishna's naughty pranks, and a river's wistful banks,
Rukmini's contented smile, and the forming of a riverine isle,
Sindhu Sagar's quiet crawl, and the sea level's rise and fall,
Raktabahu's brilliant ploy, and the seawater's silent decoy,
Vishnu's peaceful sleep, and the mountain's incredible steeps,
Nanda's merging with snow, and the hailstones' deadly blow,
The Pauri Bhuiyans' life of toil, and the mining of their soil,
A princess's love for her lake, and the floating *phumdi*s at stake,
Cheraman's pursuit of new beliefs, and the rise of coral reefs,
Raja Rituparna's big blunder, and the hidden limestone wonder,
Vasudeva's changed boon, and a salt lake building fortune,
Sahasrarjuna's harmful game, and how a river got its name,
Hampi's tale of warring kith, and artfully weathered monoliths,
Rama's arrow striking land, and a stream becoming sand,
Nala's efforts broken down, and life in a faraway ghost town,
Lonasura's looming doom, and a crater caused by a boom,
Malganga's protective role, and the pebbles in a pothole,
Parvati's favourite earring, and the leap of a healing hot spring,
Dokkhin Rai's misplaced pride, and the chaos of the changing tide,
Nataraja's charming grace, and the earth's equation with space...
In all of these, movement and stillness intersperse,
For pause and play – that's the law of the universe!

Acknowledgements

For helping me bring the two diverse universes of geography and mythology together in this book, I extend my heartfelt thanks to:

Storytellers and mythologists for keeping ancient wisdom alive.

Researchers, geographers, geologists, archaeologists, anthropologists, scientists and other experts for recording the wonders of the earth.

Scientific organizations, publishing houses and online archives for providing access to research papers and journals.

My family and friends for their belief in me and my work.

The dedicated editorial manager Sini Nair and the teams at Hachette India – editorial, design, typesetting, marketing, sales, legal, accounts, all the office staff and the printing press – for playing key roles in the publishing process of this book.

A big 'Thank You!' to my exceptional editor Nimmy Chacko, for persevering to bring out the best of the writer in me; the thoughtful copy editor Rajita Gadagkar, for ironing out crinkles and simplifying the text; the amazing illustrator and designer Sharanya Kunnath, for giving new life to Indian geomythology through her art; the insightful proofreader Niyati Dhuldhoya, for refining the content; and the persistent typesetter Manmohan Kumar, for working out a clever layout to fit in all the elements.

Lastly, my deepest gratitude to every child and grown-up reading the book. I hope these stories awaken the explorer in you and fill you with awe for the gods, giants and the geography of India.

Select Bibliography and Further Reading

If you would like to know more about the myths in this book and the workings of the earth, check out these links:

Gods

The Shepherds of Shiva, Eileen McDougall, Nomadic Numerist, (https://www.nomadicnumerist.com/journal/2017/12/17/the-shepherd-of-shiva).

Fact Check: Did Rukmini come from Arunachal Pradesh? Here is what we know, Adrija Roychowdhury, *The Indian Express*, (https://indianexpress.com/article/research/fact-check-did-rukmini-come-from-arunachal-pradesh-madhavpur-mela-guajat-vijay-rupani-mahesh-sharma-5116300/).

Invasions on the Temple of Lord Jagannath, Puri, Abhimanyu Dash, *Orissa Review*, (http://magazines.odisha.gov.in/Orissareview/2011/july/engpdf/82-89.pdf).

History, Cheraman Juma Masjid, (https://www.cheramanmosque.com/history.php).

Land of eighteen tides and one goddess, Malay Dasgupta, People's Archive of Rural India (PARI), (https://ruralindiaonline.org/en/articles/land-of-eighteen-tides-and-one-goddess/).

About the Temple, Chidambaram Nataraja Temple, (http://www.chidambaramnataraja.org/about_temple.html).

Giants

Did a Comet Cause the Great Flood?, Scott Carney, *Discover Magazine*, (https://www.discovermagazine.com/planet-earth/did-a-comet-cause-the-great-flood).

The Yeti: Asia's Abominable Snowman, Benjamin Radford, Live Science, (https://www.livescience.com/25072-yeti-abominable-snowman.html).

Rahasya: Patal Bhuvaneshwar – a mysterious cave, NewsNation, (https://www.dailymotion.com/video/x7tve6m).

Dinosaur fossils found in Narmada Valley – Ambreesh Mishra, *India Today*, (https://www.indiatoday.in/india/north/story/dinosaur-fossils-found-in-narmada-valley-69680-2010-03-17).

Geography and Geomythology

What is Gondwana?, Stephanie Pappas, Live Science (https://www.livescience.com/37285-gondwana.html).

About Comets, USRA Lunar and Planetary Institute, (https://www.lpi.usra.edu/education/explore/comets/background/).

An ancient harbour at Dwarka: Study based on the recent underwater explorations, A. S. Gaur, Sundaresh, and Sila Tripati, *Current Science*, (https://wwwops.currentscience.ac.in/Downloads/article_id_086_09_1256_1260_0.pdf).

Chilika Development Authority, (http://www.chilika.com/).

Fight for Khandadhar, Anupam Chakravartty, *Down To Earth*, (https://magazine.outlookindia.com/story/the-death-of-a-waterfall/281092).

The Paudi Bhuyan, Prof. A. B. Ota and Shri Trilochan Sahoo, Scheduled Castes & Scheduled Tribes Research and Training Institute (SCSTRTI), Bhubaneshwar, (https://repository.tribal.gov.in/bitstream/123456789/73840/1/SCST_2010_handbook_0005.pdf).

People of the Lake: A conversation with Asem Chanu Manimala on the occasion of International Day of the World's Indigenous Peoples 2020, *PangSau Collective*, (https://pangsau.com/2020/08/09/people-of-the-lake-a-conversation-with-asem-chanu-manimala-on-the-occasion-of-international-day-of-the-worlds-indigenous-people-2020/).

How Do Coral Reefs Form?, National Oceanic and Atmospheric Administration, U.S. Department of Commerce, (https://oceanservice.noaa.gov/education/tutorial_corals/coral04_reefs.html).

Playas, USGS Western Region Geology and Geophysics Science Center, (https://pubs.usgs.gov/of/2004/1007/playas.html).

Vijayanagara Research Project, Penn Museum, (https://www.penn.museum/sites/VRP/default.html).

Climatic and hydrological changes created Thar desert, Chaitanya Kalbag, *India Today*, (https://www.indiatoday.in/magazine/heritage/story/19820430-climatic-and-hydrological-changes-created-thar-desert-771727-2013-10-15).

Deccan Traps, Volcano World, Oregon State University, (http://volcano.oregonstate.edu/deccan-traps).

Nighoj Ranjan Khalge Kund, Travel IJ, (https://www.youtube.com/watch?v=D6F_sFHcxkA).

Hot Water Springs in India, Staff Reporter, *Geography and You*, (https://geographyandyou.com/hot-water-springs-in-india/).

Geomythology: geological origins of myths and legends, Dorothy B. Vitaliano, Geological Society, London, Special Publications, (https://sp.lyellcollection.org/content/specpubgsl/273/1/1.full.pdf).

Geomythology of India, Dornadula Chandrasekharam, Geological Society, London, Special Publications, (https://www.researchgate.net/publication/249551803_Geomythology_of_India).

Geological Survey of India, (https://www.gsi.gov.in/).